Story of O

Story of O

Pauline Réage

Translated by John Paul Hand

LIBRARY OF EROTIC CLASSICS

1

The Lovers of Roissy

One day her lover takes O for a walk, but this time in a part of the city—the Parc Montsouris, the Parc Monceau—where they've never been before. After they've strolled a while along the paths, after they've sat down together side by side on a bench near the grass, and then moved on toward the edge of the park, at an intersection where in the past there never used to be any taxi stand, they see a car, at that corner, that looks like a taxi, for it has a meter.

"Get in," he says.

She gets in. It's late in the afternoon, it's autumn, and she is wearing what she always wears: high heels, a suit with a pleated skirt, a silk blouse and no hat. But she has on long gloves reaching up to the sleeves of her jacket, and in her leather handbag she's got her papers, her compact and lipstick.

The taxi drives away, very slowly; the man next to her has not said a word to the driver. But on the right, and the left, he pulls down the window shades, and the one on the back window, too. Thinking that he is about to kiss her, or that he wants her to caress him, she has slipped off her gloves. Instead, he says: "Let me take your bag, it's in your way."

She gives it to him, he puts it beyond her reach, then adds:

"You have too much clothing on. Unhook your stockings, roll them down to above your knees," and he gives her some garters to hold the stockings in place. It isn't easy in the car, which is going faster now, and she's afraid the driver might turn around. But she finally manages anyhow; it's a strange, uncomfortable feeling, the contact of the silk of her slip on her naked and free legs, and the loose garters sliding back and forth across her skin.

"Undo your garterbelt," he says, "and take off your panties."

There's nothing to that; all she has to do is reach the hook and raise a little in the back. He takes the garter belt from her, takes the panties, opens her bag, puts them inside; then he says:

"You're not to sit on your slip or your skirt. Pull them up and sit right on the seat. The seat is fake leather, slick and cold, it's a very strange feeling, the way it sticks and clings to her thighs. Then he says:

"Now put your gloves back on."

The taxi is moving right along, and she doesn't dare ask why René is so quiet, so still, or what all this means to him, having her there so motionless and silent, so naked and so vulnerable, though so thoroughly gloved, in a black car going God knows where. He hasn't told her to do anything, and yet, on the other hand, he hasn't forbidden her to do anything; but she doesn't dare cross her legs or sit with them pressed together. She rests her gloved hands on the seat, pushing down; bracing herself.

4

"Here we are," he says all of a sudden. The taxi comes to a stop on a lovely avenue, under a tree—they are plane trees—in front of a small mansion, you could just see it, nestled between the courtyard and garden, the way Faubourg Saint-Germain mansions are. There's no streetlight nearby, it is dark inside the taxi. Outside rain is falling.

"Don't move," René says. "Don't move."

He extends his hand toward the neck of her blouse, unties the bow at the throat, then unbuttons the buttons. She leans forward ever so slightly, believing he is about to caress her breasts. But no. He's got a small penknife out, he's only groping for the shoulder straps of her brassiere, which he cuts. Then he removes the brassiere. He has closed her blouse again and now, underneath, her breasts are free and naked, like her belly and thighs are naked and free, like the rest of her, from waist to knee.

"Listen," he says. "You're ready. Here is where I leave you. You're going to get out, go to the door and ring the bell. Someone will open the door; whoever it is, do as you're told. Do it right away and willingly, or else they'll make you. If you don't obey at once, they'll make you. No, you don't need your bag any more. You don't need anything, you're just the girl I'm furnishing. Yes, certainly, I'll be there. Now go."

Another version of the same beginning was simpler and more direct. Similarly dressed, the young woman was driven off in a car by her lover and by a second man, an unknown friend of his. The stranger drove, the lover was seated beside the young woman, and the one who did the talking, the unknown stranger in the front seat, explained to the young woman that her lover's task was to prepare her, that he was going to tie her hands behind her back, unfasten her garterbelt, her panties, and her brassiere, and blindfold her. Afterward she would be taken to the chateau where she would receive instructions in due course, as required. And indeed, once undressed and bound in this manner, and after about a thirty-minute drive, she was helped out of the car and guided up a few steps, still blind-folded. She passed through one or two doors and then found herself alone, the blindfold removed, standing in a dark room where she was left for half an hour, maybe an hour, even two—I don't know—but it seemed as though it were forever. When the door finally opened and the light turned on, you could see that she'd been waiting in a room, an ordinary room, comfortable, yet strange. There was a thick carpet on the floor, but not a stick of furniture. The walls were lined with closets. Two girls opened the door—two pretty young chambermaids, with long, light, full skirts that came down to the floor, tight bodices that made the bust rise and swell and that were laced or hooked in back, lace kerchiefs at the neck, with matching elbow-length lace gloves. Their eyes and mouths were highly painted. Each girl wore a collar around her neck, and bracelets on her wrists.

And then I know that they released O's hands, which till then had been tied behind her back, and told her to undress. They were going to bathe her and make her up. But they made her stand still; they did everything for her: they stripped her and put her clothes away neatly in one of the cupboards. They did not let her bathe herself, they washed her themselves and set her hair just as hairdressers would have, making her sit in one of those large chairs that tilt backward when your hair is being washed and then

6

straighten up again when the drier is applied. That took at least an hour; more than an hour actually. She was seated naked on the chair, and they forbade her either to cross her legs or press them together. And since on the opposite wall there was a mirror that went from floor to ceiling right in front of her, every time she glanced up she caught sight of herself, of her open body.

When she was properly made up, her eyelids lightly shadowed, her mouth bright red, the point and halo of her nipples rouged, the lips of her sex reddened, a lingering scent applied to her armpits and pubis, to the crease between her buttocks, beneath her breasts and on the palms of her hands, she was led into a room where a three-sided mirror and, behind it, a fourth mirror on the opposite wall, enabled her to see her own reflected image. She was told to sit on a hassock placed between the mirrors, and wait. The hassock was upholstered with prickly black fur; the rug was black, the walls were red. She wore red slippers. Set in one of the little bedroom walls was a casement window looking out onto a magnificent but somber formal garden. The rain had stopped and the trees were swaying in the wind, while the moon raced high among the clouds.

I don't know how long she remained in the red bedroom, if she was really alone, as she thought, for someone might have been watching her through a peephole set somewhere in the wall. What I do know is that when the two chambermaids returned, one was carrying a dressmaker's tapemeasure and the other a basket. With them came a man wearing a long purple robe with sleeves cut wide at the shoulder and gathered at the wrist. As he walked, the robe flared open at the waist, and you could see that he was wearing some kind of tights which covered his legs and thighs but left his sex exposed. It was the sex that O saw first, then the whip, made of leather thongs, that was stuck in his belt. Then she noticed that the man was masked in a black hood, with a piece of black gauze hiding his eyes—and finally she noticed the fine black kid gloves he was wearing.

He ordered her not to move, and told the women to hurry. The one with the tape measured O's neck and wrists. Although somewhat small, her sizes were in no way out of the ordinary, and they had no trouble finding a suitable collar and bracelets from the assortment contained in the basket. Both collar and bracelets were made of several layers of thin leather, the whole being no thicker than a finger, fitted with a catch that worked automatically, like a padlock, and which required a key to be opened. Right next to the catch, and imbedded in the leather, was a snug-fitting metal ring. Snug, but not so tight as to chafe or break the skin.

After they had been set in place, the man told her to get up. He sat down on the fur-covered hassock and made her approach until she was touching his knees. He slipped his gloved hand between her thighs and over her breasts, and explained to her that she would be presented that same evening after she had dined alone.

Still naked, she took her meal alone in a kind of small cabin; an invisible hand passed the plates to her through a small window. When she had finished eating, the two women came for her again. In the bedroom, they had her put her hands behind her back and fastened them there by the rings of her wristbands. They draped a long red cape over her shoulders and fastened it to the ring set in her collar. The cape covered her completely, but with her hands

8

behind her back, she couldn't prevent it from opening as she walked. One woman preceded her and opened the doors; the other followed, and shut them behind her. They filed through a vestibule, through two drawing rooms, and went into the library where four men were having coffee. They wore the same flowing robes as the first man she had seen, but were not masked. And yet, O did not have time to see their faces or recognize whether her lover was there (he was), for one of the men shone a light on her face, blinding her. Everyone stood in silence, the women on either side, the men in front, studying her. Then the light was switched off and the women left. But once again a blindfold had been placed over O's eyes. Stumbling, she was made to advance and could sense that she was standing in front of the fire around which the four men had been seated. In the silence, she could hear the soft crackling of the logs and feel the heat. She was facing the fire. Two hands lifted away her cape, two others checked the clasp on her wristbands and descended the length of her back and buttocks. The hands were not gloved, and one of them simultaneously penetrated her in two places—so suddenly that she let out a cry. Someone laughed. Another said:

"Turn her around so we can see her breasts and belly."

She was turned around, and now she felt the glow of the fire on her back. A hand seized one of her breasts, a mouth closed on the nipple of her other breast. But suddenly she lost her balance and fell backward into someone's arms. At the same time, her legs were spread and her lips gently opened—hair grazed the inner surface of her thighs. She heard a voice say that she ought to be made to kneel, and she was. It was painful to be in that position, especially because they did not let her bring her knees together and because, with her arms locked behind her, she was forced to lean forward. Then they let her rock back on her heels, in the position nuns take when they pray.

"You've never tied her up?"

"No, never."

"Never. Though the fact is . . . " It was her lover answering.

" . . . the fact is," said the other voice, "that if you do tie her up, or whip her a little, and if she begins to like it—then that's no good either. We'ver got to move beyond the pleasure stage. We must make the tears flow."

She was then pulled to her feet, and they were probably about to free her hands so as to tie her to some post, or to the wall, when someone interrupted, saying that he wanted to take her then and there. She was forced back down onto her knees again, but this time a hassock was placed as a support under her bosom; her hands were higher than her torso. Then one of the men gripped her buttocks and sank himself into her womb. When he was done, he yielded his place to a second. The third wanted to force his way into a narrower passage and, driving hard, wrenched a scream from her lips. When he let go of her, moaning and with tears streaming down under her blindfold, she slipped to the floor, only to discover by the pressure of someone against her face, that her mouth was not to be spared either. Finally, finished with her, they moved away, leaving her, a captive in her tawdry finery, huddled on the carpet before the fire. She heard drinks being poured, glasses tinkling, chairs scraping. They added more logs to the fire. Then her blindfold was suddenly snatched away. It was a large room. Bookcases lined the walls, dimly lit by a wall lamp and the flicker of the fire, which was burning more brightly. Two of the men were standing and smoking. Another was seated, a riding crop across his knees, and the one leaning over, caressing her breasts, was her lover. All four had taken her and she had not been able to distinguish him from the others.

They explained to her that as long as she was in this chateau it would always be this way: she would see the faces of those who violated and tormented her, but never at night, and thus she would never know which ones were responsible for the worst. When she was whipped the same would hold true, except when they wanted her to see herself being whipped, as happened to be the case now: no blindfold, but the men masked in order to be unidentifiable.

Her lover had picked her up and set her, in her red cape, on the arm of an easy chair in the corner by the chimney, so that she could hear what they had to tell her and see what they wished to show her. Her hands were still locked behind her back. She was shown the riding crop, which was black, long, and delicate, made of fine bamboo sheathed in leather, such as one sees in the windows of expensive saddlemakers' shops; the leather whip—the one she'd seen tucked in the first man's belt—was long, with six lashes each knotted at the end. There was a third whip whose numerous light cords were knotted several times and quite stiff, as if soaked in water, which in fact they had, as O was able to verify when they stroked her belly with those cords and pried open her thighs, exposing her hidden parts, let the damp, cold ends trail against the tender skin. On the console table there was a collection of keys and steel chains. Halfway up one of the library's walls ran a balcony supported by two columns. In one of these, as high up as a man standing on tip-toe could reach, was imbedded a hook. O, whose lover had taken her in his arms, with one hand under her shoulder, the other in her loins, which was burning her almost unbearably, O was told that when they unfastened her hands, which they shortly would, it would only be to attach them to this whipping post by means of those bracelets on her wrists and this steel chain. With the exception of her hands, which would be fastened a little above her head, she would be able to move, to turn around and see the strokes coming; by and large, they'd confine the whipping to her thighs and buttocks, to the space, that is between her waist and knees, in short, that part of her which had been prepared in the car when she had been made to sit naked on the seat; it was likely, however, that one of the four men would want to mark her with the riding crop, for it made fine, long, deep welts which lasted a long time. They'd go about it gradually, giving her plenty of opportunity to scream and struggle and cry to her heart's content. They'd pause to let her catch her breath, but after she'd recovered they'd start in again, judging the results not by her screams or tears but by the color and size of the welts traced in her flesh by the whips. It was called to her attention that these criteria for estimating the effectiveness of the whip, apart from their impartiality and the fact they rendered unnecessary any attempts victims might make to elicit pity by exaggerating their suffering, did not by any means preclude open-air whipping—there would indeed be a good deal of that in the part outside the chateau—or for that matter, whipping in any ordinary apartment or hotel room, provided a tight gag was employed (they produced a gag then and there and showed it to her), which, while giving free

12

rein to tears, stifles all screams and even makes moaning difficult.

They did not, however, intend to use the gag that night. On the contrary, they were eager to hear O scream, the sooner the better. Proud, she steeled herself to resist, she gritted her teeth; but not for long. They soon heard her beg for them to untie her, beg them to stop, stop for a second, for just one second. So frantically did she twist and turn to dodge the biting lashes that she almost spun in a full circle. The chain, although obviously unyielding, was nevertheless slack enough to allow her some freedom of movement. Because of her excessive writhing, her belly and the front of her thighs received almost as heavy a share of the flogging as her rear. They stopped for a moment, judging it better to tie her up against the post by means of a rope passed around her waist. They tied the rope tight, her head necessarily angled to one side of the post and her flanks jutting to the other, thereby making her rump protrude. From then on, every deliberatley aimed blow dealt her struck home. In view of the manner in which her lover had exposed her to this, O might have presumed that an appeal to his pity would have been the surest way to redouble his cruelty, so great was his pleasure in wresting, or in having the others wrest, from her these absolute proofs of his power over her. And it was in fact he who was the first to point out that the leather whip, with which they'd marked her the least (for the moistened lash had obtained results almost immediately, and the crop with the first blow struck), and hence, by employing no other, they could prolong the agony and, after brief pauses, start again almost immediatley or according to their fancy. He asked that they use only that first whip. Meanwhile, the man who

13

liked women only for what they had in common with men, seduced by the sight of that proffered behind straining at the taut rope, and made all the more tempting by its efforts to escape, requested an intermission in order to take advantage of it. He spread apart the two burning halves and penetrated, but not without difficulty, which caused him to remark that they'd have to make this thoroughfare more accessible. This could be done, they agreed, and decided that the proper measure would be taken.

The young woman, staggered, half fainting under her flowing red cape. She was then released and, before being led away to the cell where she was to stay, they sat her down in a chair by the fireside and outlined to her, in detail, all the rules she was to observe not only during her stay at the chateau but also during her everyday life once she'd returned home (not, however, that she was going to recover her former freedom). One of the men rang. The two costumed maids who had received her now appeared, carrying the clothes she was to wear, and tokens by which those who had been guests at the chateau prior to her arrival and after, would be able to recognize her when she had left. This costume was similar to that of the chambermaids'. Over a whalebone bodice, which severely constricted the waist, and over a starched linen petticoat, was worn a long, full gown, the open neck of which left the breasts, raised by the bodice, practically visible beneath a light film of lace. The petticoat and lace were white, the bodice and gown a sea green satin. When O was dressed and seated again by the fireplace, her pallor accentuated by the paleness of the gown, the two girls, who had not uttered a word, prepared to leave. As they were going, one of the men stepped foward, signaled to the one nearest the door to wait, and brought the other back toward O. He took her by the waist with one hand and raised her skirts with the other, making her turn, displaying the costume's many practical advantages, having O admire its design, and explaining that, simply by means of a belt, the skirts could be held up at any desired height, which meant that all of what was exposed was ready to hand. In fact, he added, they often had the girls stroll in the garden or move about the chateau with their skirts tucked up behind, or hitched up in front at the level of the midriff. He told the girl to show O how the skirt was to be kept in the proper position: how she was to take in the folds, roll them (like a lock of hair in a curler), keep them just so by means of a belt, the buckle exactly in front, thus leaving the way clear to the womb, or in back to expose the buttocks. In both instances, petticoat and skirt were to fall away in flowing diagonal folds. Like O, the girl's flanks bore fresh marks of the riding-crop. She left the room.

This is the speech they then delivered to O: "You are here to serve your masters. During the day, in connection with the maintenance of the household, you will perform whatever duties are assigned you, such as sweeping, putting the books back in place, arranging flowers, or waiting on table, nothing more than that. But at the first word or signal you will stop whatever you happen to be doing, and address yourself to your primary task, your only significant duty: to avail yourself to be used. Your hands are not your own, nor are your breasts; nor, above all, any of the orifices of your body, which we are at liberty to explore and, whenever we please, penetrate. In order for you to bear constantly—or as constantly as possible—in mind that you have lost all right to withhold or deny yourself, in our presence you will at all times avoid closing your lips. Nor will you ever cross your legs. Nor press your knees together (as, you recall, was forbidden you upon your arrival here), which will signify, in your view and in ours, that your mouth, your belly and your behind are constantly at our disposal. In our presence, you must never touch your breasts: your bodice lifts them supplicatingly to us, they are ours. During the day, since you will therefore be dressed, you will lift your skirt if ordered to, and whoever would have you will use you as he likes, unmasked. But he will not whip you. The whip will be applied only between dusk and dawn. But besides those whippings, which you will receive from whoever desires to whip you, you will be punished, in the form of further whipping, at night for any infraction of the rules during the day. That is, for the thoughtlessness, for being slow to oblige, for having raised your eyes on whoever speaks to you or takes you: you must never look one of us in the face. If our evening costume, what we are wearing now, leaves our sex exposed, it is not for the sake of convenience, for it would be just as convenient otherwise, but for the sake of insolence, so that your eyes will look there and nowhere else, so that you will come finally to understand that there resides your master, your lord, to whom all of you is destined, above all your lips. During the day, when we are dressed in normal attire and you as you are now, you will observe the same rule, and when requested you will simply open your clothing and later close it again when we have finished with you. Also, at night, you will have only your lips with which to honor us, and also your widespread thighs, since, at night, you will have your hands tied behind your back

16

and you will be naked, as you were when you were brought here a short while ago. You will not be blindfolded except when you are to be maltreated and, now that you have seen yourself being beaten, when you are to be whipped. One thing more: if it were advisable that you accustom yourself to be whipped—and it shall be frequent, daily, so long as you remain here—it is less for our pleasure than for your instruction. This may be stressed by the fact that, on those nights when no one wants you, you may expect a visit from the valet whom we have appointed to do the job: he will enter your solitary cell and mete out to you what you need to receive and which we are not in the mood to bestow. Actually, the point of these procedures, as well as of the chain which will be affixed to your collar, is more to confine you to your bed for several hours every day, than to make you suffer pain, scream, or shed tears. This pain will enforce upon you the idea that you are subject to constraint and to teach you that you belong completely to something which is apart from and outside yourself. When you leave here, you will be wearing an iron ring on your third finger, by which others will recognize you. You will by then have learned to obey those who wear the same token—upon seeing it, they will know that you are constantly naked beneath your skirt, however comely or ordinary your dress, and that this nudity is for them. Anyone who finds you uncooperative will bring you back here. Now you will be shown to your cell."

While these words were being spoken to O, the two women who had come to dress her were standing on either side of the post where she had been whipped, without touching it, as though it frightened them, or (which was more likely) as though they had been forbidden to

17

touch it. When the man had concluded, they moved toward O, who understood that she was to get up and follow them. She got to her feet, gathered her skirts in her arms to keep from stumbling, for she wasn't used to long dresses nor to managing in these thick-soled, very high-heeled clogs which only a single, broad strap of satin, of the same green as her gown, prevented from slipping off. Stooping to gather her skirts, she cast a quick glance around. The women were waiting, the men had shifted their attention elsewhere. Her lover, seated on the floor, his back propped against the ottoman over which she'd been thrust earlier in the evening, his legs drawn up and his elbows on his knees, was toying with the leather whip. At the first step she took to overtake the women, the edge of her skirt grazed him. He looked up, smiling, calling her name. Then he too rose to his feet. Softly he caressed her hair, ran the tip of his finger softly along her eyebrows, and softly kissed her lips. He gazed at her and, rather loudly, said that he loved her. Trembling, O was terrified to hear herself saying: "I love you," and it was true. He pressed her to him and said: "My love, my darling," then kissed her chin, kissed her neck, kissed the curve of her cheek, for she had let her head fall on the shoulder of his purple robe. Murmuring now, he repeated that he loved her and, even more softly, said: "Now kneel down, caress me, kiss me." He pushed her away, motioned the women back, and leaned back against the console. He was tall, but the console was not very high, and his long legs, sheathed in the same purple as her dress, were slightly bent. The open robe hung like a drapery. The top of the console, pushing against his buttocks from behind, thrust forward his heavy sex and the light fleece above it. The three men drew near.

O knelt on the rug, her green skirt spread around her like a pool. Her bodice held her breasts, the nipples visible at the level of her lover's knees. "A little more light," said one of the men. As they directed the beam so that it would fall directly on his sex and on the face of his mistress, which was almost touching it, and on her hands, which were already caressing him, René said: "Say it again: 'I love you.'" O said: "I love you," with such delight that she scarcely dared touch the tip of his sex, still protected by its sheath of soft skin. The three men who were smoking, commented on her movements, on the way her mouth closed over and worked at the sex it had seized and along whose length it moved rhythmically back and forth, on the tears that came to her eyes every time the swollen member struck the back of her throat and made her choke, to shudder as though from an imminent nausea. It was with her mouth still half-gagged by the hardened flesh that filled it that she murmured again the words: "I love you." The two women had stationed themselves on either side of René who, with one arm around each of their shoulders, had lowered himself toward O. She heard the remarks being made by the people present, but listened through them for her lover's moans, caressing him carefully, with infinite respect, slowly, the way she knew he liked it. O was aware of the splendor of her mouth, of its beauty, since her love deigned to enter it, since he deigned to make a spectacle of its caresses, since he deigned to discharge into it. She received him as one receives a god, heard his cry, heard the others laugh, and when she had received his seed, she fell and lay with her face against the floor. The two women helped her to her feet and this time led her away.

19

The clogs clacked on the red tiles of the hallways; they passed door after door: discreet and clean, all these doors had tiny keyholes, tiny locks, like the doors of the rooms in the best hotels. O was working up the courage to ask whether all these room were inhabited, and if so by whom, when one of her companions, whose voice she had not previously heard told her: "You're in the red wing. Your valet's name is Pierre."

"What valet?" O asked, impressed by the gentleness of the voice. "And what is your name?"

"Andrée."

"I'm Jeanne," said the second.

The first continued: "He has the keys, it is he who will chain and unchain you, who will whip you when you are to be punished or when the others haven't the time or inclination to do it themselves."

"I was in the red wing last year," said Jeanne. "Pierre had already arrived by then. He often came at night; the valets have the keys. They have the right to use any of us who are in their section whenever they wish."

O was about to ask what Pierre was like. But she did not have time to: for at the turn of the hallway they halted before a door identical to all the others. Between this door and the next one to it was a small bench. Sitting on it was a peasant, a squat, ruddy-faced man, his hair close-cropped, with little deep set black eyes and rolls of fat on his neck. He was dressed like an operetta valet: in a ruffled shirt whose lace collar protruded from a red domestic's jacket under which he had on a black waistcoat. His breeches were black, his stockings white, and he was wearing patent-leather shoes with buckles. He too carried a many-thonged leather whip at his belt. Red hairs covered the backs of his hands. He stood up, drew a master key from a pocket in his waistcoat, unlocked the door, ushered the three women in, saying: "I'm locking the door. Ring when you're done."

The cell was very small, although it was actually made up of two rooms. With the hall door shut they found themselves in an antechamber opening into the cell proper; inside this room, and next to the entrance, was another door leading to the bathroom. At the far end, as one entered, was a window. Against the wall to the left, between the doors and the window, was the headboard of a large square bed, quite low and covered with furs. There was no other furniture, no mirror. The walls were bright red, the carpet was black. Andrée pointed out that the bed was less a bed than a mattressed platform covered with a spread made of imitation fur. Flat and hard too, the pillowcase was of the same material. The only object to be seen on an otherwise bare wall, at about the same distance above the bed as the hook in the post was above the floor of the library, was a large gleaming steel ring from which descended a long steel chain, its lower end forming a little pile of links on the bed, finishing in a padlocked catch. The whole thing looked like a drapery, neatly drawn back and held by a curtain loop.

"We must have you take your bath," said Jeanne. "I'll unfasten your dress."

The only noticeable features about the bathroom were the Turkish toilet, set in the corner nearest the door, and the presence of mirrors, which covered every wall. Jeanne and Andrée did not allow O to enter until she was naked. They laid her dress in the closet next to the basin where her clogs and red cape had already been put away, and stayed with her so that when she squatted down over the porcelain toilet she discovered herself surrounded by as many reflected images, feeling as exposed as when she had been forced by unknown hands in the library.

"Not now," said Jeanne. "Wait till Pierre comes. Then you can look."

"Why wait for Pierre?"

"When he comes to chain you he may make you squat."

O felt herself grow pale. "But why?" she asked.

"You'll just have to," Jeanne replied. "But you're lucky."

"Why lucky?"

"Your lover brought you here, didn't he?"

"Yes," O said.

"Then they'll be much harder on you."

"I don't understand . . . ."

"You will very soon. I'll ring for Pierre. We'll come to get you tomorrow morning."

Andrée smiled as she left; Jeanne, before following her out, caressed the tips of O's breasts. O, quite taken aback, stood at the foot of the bed. Apart from the leather collar and wristbands, hardened and constricted by the water from her bath, she was naked.

"Ah, behold the lovely lady," said the valet as he entered, and caught hold of both her hands. He slipped the catch of one wrist band into the other, snapped them shut, then, raising her hands, he secured them to the hook of her collar. Which left her with her hands pressed palm to palm at the level of her neck, as if in prayer. All that remained now was to chain her to the wall, with the chain that was coiled on the bed. He unlocked the hasp at the chain's upper end and made some adjustments, shortening it. O had to move closer to the head of the bed, whereupon

22

Pierre made her lie down. The chain clicked through the ring until at last the young woman could only move to the right or left on the bed, or stand up on either side of the headboard. Since the chain was pulling the collar behind and, at the same time, her hands tended to pull it around to the front, an equilibrium was established, bringing her joined hands to lie on her left shoulder, toward which her head was also leaning. The valet pulled the black coverlet up over O, but not until he had first drawn her legs up toward her chest and gazed for a moment at the cleft between her thighs. He did not touch her again, did not say a word; he turned out the light—the lamp was on the wall between the two doors—and left.

Lying on her left side, alone in the darkness and the silence, hot between the two layers of fur, O wondered why such a great flush of sweetness mingled with the terror inside her, or why terror should have such a sweet taste. She realized that, in large measure, her distress resulted from her inability to use her hands; not that her hands could have defended her (did she indeed really desire to defend herself?), but, with her hands free, she would at least have been able to make a gesture of self-defense, a slight attempt to push away the hands that had seized her flesh from the whip. They had taken her hands from her, freed her of them; her body under the fur, her own body was inaccessible to her. How strange it was, not to be able to touch one's own knees, or the opening of one's own womb. Her lips, the burning lips between her legs, were forbidden her, and perhaps burned because she knew they were open, awaiting whoever might happen to want them: openly awaiting Pierre, if he cared to enter. She was amazed to find that the memory of the whip could leave her so untroubled, so serene, whereas the thought that she would probably never know which of the four men had twice taken her behind, or know if it had indeed been the same man who had done it both times, or even know whether it might not have been her lover—this thought distressed her greatly. She turned slightly on her belly for a moment, remembering that her lover loved the furrow between her buttocks, and that he had never before this evening (if it had been he) penetrated her there. Did she dare hope that it had been René? Could she ask him? Ah, no, never. Once again she saw the hand which in the car had taken her garter belt and panties from her, and stretched her stockings while she rolled them down just above the knee. So striking was the image that she forgot her hands were bound, and made the chain grate. And why, if the memory of her lashing weighed so lightly upon her, should the mere thought, the mere sight of the whip, the very word itself, make her heart beat wildly and make her eyes shut with terror? She did not stop to consider whether it was only terror; a panic seized her. There would be a jerk on her chain, she would be hauled down, made to stand up on her bed and she would be whipped, her belly glued to the wall, she would be whipped, and whipped, and whipped—the word whirled in her brain. Pierre would whip her, Jeanne had said so. You're lucky, Jeanne had repeated, they'll be much harder on you. What had she meant by that? Then she ceased to be conscious of anything except the collar, the bracelets, and the chain; her body began to drift away, soon she would understand. And she fell asleep.

In the final hours of the night, when it is darkest, and

coldest just before dawn, Pierre reappeared. He switched on the bathroom light, leaving the door open, so that a square of light fell on the center of the bed where O's slender body was curled up, making a small mound under the blanket. This Pierre silently pulled away. Since O was lying on her left side, her face toward the window, her knees slightly drawn up, it was her white flanks reclining on the black fur that met his gaze. He removed the pillow from under her head; and he said politely: "Would you please stand up," and when, helping herself by holding onto the chain, she had gotten to her knees, he took her elbows to help her the rest of the way. She faced the wall, her forearms and elbows flush against it. The light cast on the bed was faint, since the bed was black, and while it made her body visible, his gestures were not. Without being able to see, she guessed he was loosening the chain and refastening it by another link, to keep her upright. By the pressure on her neck she felt the chain grow taut. Her bare feet rested flat on the bed. Nor did she see that, instead of the leather whip, he was carrying on his belt a black riding crop similar to the one with which she had been struck earlier, but only twice, and they had not been hard, softer than the cuts she'd received at the pillory. Pierre's left hand settled on her waist, she sensed the mattress give a little, for he had put his right foot on it; he was bracing himself. At the same time, O heard a whistle in the semi-darkness, and she felt a terrible blaze rip across her flanks, and she screamed. Pierre flogged her with all his might. He did not wait for her screams to subside, and four times over started in again, taking care to deliver the blows either above or below the spot he had been working on before, so that the pattern of welts would be distinct. Even after Pierre had stopped she went on screaming, and her tears continued to flow down into her open mouth.

"Kindly turn around," he said. And when she, half-fainting, failed to respond, he seized her haunches without letting go of the crop, whose handle grazed her waist. When he had turned her around, he moved away slightly; then with all his might, he swung his crop against the front of her thighs. The whole thing had lasted five minutes. When he had gone, after turning out the light and closing the bathroom door, O, moaning in the darkness, dangling at the end of her chain, swayed to and fro against the wall. She tried to calm herself, and lay still against the bright percale covering the wall, the cloth cool against her tortured flesh, watching dawn try to pierce the gloom. The long window toward which she was turned, for she was leaning on one hip, looked east. That window, which extended from floor to ceiling, was uncurtained, although framed by the same red material adorning the wall and which, in the embrasure on either side, fell in heavy folds. O watched the pale dawn slowly break through the night mists still trailing on the clustered asters outside at the foot of the window, the thinning mist finally disclosing a poplar tree. Yellow leaves drifted down in slow spirals from time to time, even though there was no wind. From the window, after the bed of purple asters, a lawn was visible, and beyond it a pathway. And now it was broad daylight, it had been a long time since O had last stirred. A gardener came along the path pushing a wheelbarrow. Its iron wheel could be heard squeaking on the gravel. Had he come nearer, to rake up the leaves fallen by the asters, that window was so large and the room so small and brightly lit that he would have seen O, chained and naked, and the marks the

26

riding crop had left on her thighs. The welts had swollen and formed narrow ridges of a much darker red than the red of the wall. Where was her lover sleeping, as he loved to sleep on quiet mornings? In which room, in what bed? Did he know to what tortures he had delivered her? Was it he who had decided them? O's thoughts turned to those prisoners depicted in the engravings in history books, men who had been chained and whipped a long time ago, centuries ago, and who were dead. She did not want to die, but if torture were the price she was to have to pay for her lover's love, then she only hoped he was happy because of what she had endured. And she waited, soft and silent, for them to take her back to him.

None of the women there possessed keys either to the doors or to the chains, to the collars or the wristbands, but every man carried a bunch of keys; three in all, one for all the doors, another for all the locks, the last for all the collars and bracelets. The valets had keys too. But now that it was morning, the valets who had been on night duty were asleep, and it was one of the masters, or some other valet, who would come to open the locks. The man who entered O's cell was dressed in a suede jacket, riding breeches and boots. She did not recognize him. First, he unlocked the wall chain, and O was able to lie down on her bed. Before freeing her wrists, he passed his hand between her thighs, the way the masked, gloved man she had seen first in the small red room had done. Perhaps this was he. He had a bony, sharp-featured face, the steady gaze one sees in the portraits of old Huguenots, and his hair was grizzled. O met his stare for what seemed to her an endless period, then suddenly froze; she remembered that one was forbidden to look at the masters anywhere above the belt. She shut her eyes, but it was too late, and she heard him laugh as he set about freeing her hands at last. "Punishment for that will come after dinner," he said.

He spoke to Andrée and Jeanne, who had come in with him and were waiting on either side of the bed. After which he left. Andrée picked up the pillow from where it had fallen to the floor and straightened the coverlet which Pierre had turned down when he had come to whip O; meanwhile Jeanne wheeled in a serving table which she set beside the bed. On it were coffee, milk, sugar, bread, butter, and croissants. "Eat quickly," said Andrée, "it's nine o'clock. Afterward you can sleep till noon, and when you hear the bell it will be time to get up and get ready for lunch. You'll do your own bathing and arrange your hair yourself. I'll come to make you up and lace your bodice."

"You won't be on duty until the afternoon," said Jeanne. "In the library: to serve coffee, liqueurs, and take care of the fire."

"But what about you?" O asked.

"We're only supposed to look after you for the first twenty-four hours of your stay. After that you'll be alone, and only men will deal with you. We won't be able to talk to you, and you won't be able to talk to us."

"Please stay, please, and tell me . . . . " But O's words were cut off by the opening of the door: it was her lover, and he was not alone.

It was René, dressed the way he was when he got out of bed and lit his first cigarette of the day. He was in striped pajamas and a blue wool bathrobe, the one with the quilted silk lapels they'd chosen together the year before. And his slippers were shabby, badly moth-eaten; she would have to buy him a new pair. The two women disappeared without a sound, except for the rustling of silk when they lifted their skirts (all the skirts trailed on the floor); the clogs couldn't be heard on the carpet.

O, who was sitting rather precariously half on and half off the bed, one leg hanging over the edge, the other tucked up toward her body, didn't budge, although the cup suddenly began to shake in her hand and she dropped her croissant.

"Pick it up," René said.

That was the first thing he had said. She posed the cup on the table, retrieved the partly eaten croissant, and put it by the cup. A large croissant crumb remained on the floor, touching O's bare foot. This time René stooped down and picked it up. Then he sat down next to O, pulled her back onto the bed, and kissed her. She asked him if he loved her. "Oh, yes! I do love you," he answered. Then he got up, pulled her up too, and gently pressed his cool palms, then his lips to her welts.

Since the other man had come in with her lover, O wasn't sure whether or not she was allowed to look at him. He had turned his back for a moment and was smoking near the door. What followed could not have been an encouragement to her.

"Come here, let's have a look at you," her lover said and, having guided her to the foot of the bed, remarked to his companion that he had indeed been correct, expressed his thanks, adding that it only seemed fair that he, the stranger, be the first to take her if he were so inclined.

The stranger, whom she still dared not look at, after having run his hands over her breasts and down her buttocks, asked her to spread her legs.

"Do as you're told," said René, against whose chest her

29

back was resting and who was holding her erect. His right hand was caressing one of her breasts, his left hand held her shoulder. The stranger had seated himself on the edge of the bed. He had seized and gradually parted the lips guarding the entrance, using her pubic hair to ease his task. René pushed in an effort to facilitate the task, as soon as he understood what the other was after, and slipped his right arm around her waist, thus improving the accessibility.

This caress, to which she had never before acceded without a struggle and without an overwhelming feeling of shame, and from which she would escape as quickly as she could, so quickly in fact that she scarcely had a chance to be affected by it, was a caress that seemed a sacrilege to her, because it seemed sacrilegious that her lover be on his knees when by rights she ought to be on hers—suddenly, she sensed that she was not going to escape from this caress, and she saw herself doomed. For she moaned when this unknown man's mouth pushed aside the folds of flesh whence the inner corolla emerges, moaned when those stranger lips abruptly set her afire, then retreated to let his tongue's hot tip burn her even more. She moaned louder when his lips seized her anew; she felt the hidden point harden and protrude, to be taken between teeth and tongue in a long sucking bite that held her, and held her, and would not let her go. She lost her footing and found herself on her back, René's mouth on her mouth; his two hands pinned her shoulders to the bed while two other hands, gripping her calves, were raising and opening her legs. Her own hands, which were behind and under her back (for at the same time he had thrust her toward the stranger, René had bound her wrists by locking the two wristbands together), her hands were brushed by the sex of the man who was caressing himself in the crease between her buttocks. That sex now rose and struck swiftly into the depths of her belly. In answer to that first blow she cried out as though under the lash, then acknowledged each succeeding blow with a cry, and her lover bit her mouth. Then the man suddenly withdrew, fell backward as though struck by lightning, and from his throat there also came a cry.

René freed O's hands, eased her along the bed, and tucked her in under the blanket. The stranger got up and René escorted him to the door. In a flash, O saw herself immolated, annihilated, cursed. She had moaned under the stranger's mouth as she never had under René's, cried out before the onslaught of the stranger's member as never her lover had made her cry. She felt profaned and guilty. If he were to abandon her, she would not blame him. But no, the door swung closed, René was still there, was staying with her, he walked toward her, lay down beside her, beneath the blanket, slipped into her wet, hot belly, and holding her in this embrace, said to her: "I love you. After I've also given you to the valets, I'll come some night and lash you till the blood flows."

The sun had dissipated the mists, and was flooding the room. But it wasn't until the midday bell rang that they awoke.

O did not know what to do. Her lover was there, just as near, just as relaxed and abandoned as in the bed of the low-ceilinged room where, almost every night since they had been living together, he'd come to sleep with her. It was a big, four-poster mahogany bed, but without the canopy, and the posts at the head were taller than those at

31

the foot. He always slept to her left and, whenever he awoke, even in the middle of the night, he would always reach a hand toward her legs. That was why she never wore anything but a nightgown or, if pajamas, she never wore the bottoms.

He did that now too; she took his hand and kissed it, not daring to ask him anything. But he spoke. He slipped two fingers between her neck and the collar, and told her that from now on she would be shared by him and by others of his choosing, and by still others whom he didn't know who were affiliated with the society that shared the chateau, as she had been the previous evening. He told her that she belonged to, and was ultimately dependable on, him, and only him, even if she were to receive orders from others than he, no matter whether he were present or absent, for as a matter of principle he concurred in whatever she might be required to do, or whatever might be inflicted on her; and that it was he who possessed and enjoyed her through those into whose hands he surrendered her, from the simple fact that she was surrendered to them by him. She must submit to them all, and greet them with the same respect she greeted him, as if they were so many images of him. Thus he would possess her as a god possesses his creatures whom he lays hands on in the guise of some monster or bird, some invisible spirit or state of ecstasy. He did not want to leave her. The more he subjected her to, the more important to him she would become. The fact that he gave her to others was a proof to him and as well to her, that she belonged to him. He gave her so as to reclaim her immediately, reclaim her enriched a hundredfold in his eyes, as is a common object that has served some divine purpose and thereby become sanctified. For a long time he had wanted to prostitute her, and was delighted to discover that the pleasure he reaped from it was even greater than he had dared hope, and increased his attachment to her, as it did hers to him, and that attachment would be all the greater the more her prostitution humiliated and debased her. Since she loved him, she had no choice but to love whatever emanated from him. O listened and trembled with happiness; since he loved her, she trembled, acquiescent. In all likelihood he sensed her consent, for he continued:

"It's because it's so easy for you to consent that I want from you something you can't possibly agree to, even if you agree in advance, even if you say yes now and imagine that you are actually capable of submitting to it. You won't be able to keep yourself from saying no when the time comes. When it does, it won't matter what you say, you'll be made to submit, not only for the sake of the incomparable pleasure I or others will derive from your submission, but so that you will be made aware of what has been done to you."

O was about to reply that she was his slave and revelled in that bondage; but he stopped her:

"Yesterday you were told that, so long as you are in this chateau, you are neither to look a man in the face nor speak to him. Nor must you look at me or speak to me any more. You must simply be still and obey. I love you. Now get up. From now on, as long as you're here, you must not open your mouth again in the presence of a man, except to scream or to caress."

So O got up. René remained stretched out on the bed. She bathed, and arranged her hair. The tepid water made her bruised buttocks shiver, she had to sponge herself gen-

33

tly but not rub, to avoid reviving the burning pain. She painted her mouth, but not her eyes, powdered herself and, still naked but with her eyes lowered, came back into the room.

René was looking at Jeanne, who had entered and was standing at the head of the bed, she too with lowered eyes, silent. He told her to dress O. Jeanne took the green satin bodice, the white petticoat, the gown, the green clogs and, having hooked up O's bodice in front, began to lace it up tight in the back. The bodice was stout and whaleboned, long and stiff, something from the days when wasp waists were in fashion, and was fitted with gussets to support the breasts. The tighter it was drawn, the more prominently O's breasts rose, thrust upward by the gussets, and the more prominently her nipples were displayed. At the same time, as her waist was constricted, her womb and buttocks were made to arch out. The strange thing is that this armor was exceedingly comfortable and, to some extent relaxing. It made one stand up very straight, but, without one being able to tell precisely how or why, unless it was by contrast, it increased one's consciousness of the freedom, or rather the availability, of the parts it left unrestricted. The full skirt and the neckline, plunging from her shoulders to the whole width of her breasts, looked to the girl wearing it less like a protective device than a provocative piece of clothing, a mechanism for display. When Jeanne had tied a bow in the laces and knotted it for good measure, O took her gown from the bed. It was a one-piece dress, the petticoat tucked inside the skirt like an interchangeable lining, and the bodice, cross-laced in front and tied in back by a second series of laces, was thus, depending on how tightly it was done up, able to reproduce more or less exactly the delicate contours of the bust. Jeanne had laced it very tight, and O caught a glimpse of herself in the mirror through the open door to the bathroom, her slender torso rising like a flower from the mass of the green satin billowing, at her hips, as if she were wearing a hoop skirt. The two women were standing side by side. Jeanne reached up to correct a wrinkle in the sleeve of the green gown, and her breasts stirred beneath her fringe, breasts whose nipples were long, whose halos were brown. Her gown was of yellow faille.

René, who had approached the two women, said to O: "Look." And to Jeanne: "Lift your dress." With both hands she lifted the stiff crackling silk and the linen lining, to reveal a golden belly, honey thighs and knees, and a tight black triangle. René put out his hand and probed it slowly, his other hand exciting the nipple of one breast, till it grew hard and yet darker.

"That's simply so you can see," he told O. O saw. She saw his ironic but concentrated face, his eyes intently scanning Jeanne's half-open mouth and her throat, circled by the leather collar. What pleasure could she, O, give him, that this woman or some other could not?

"Hadn't you thought of that?" he asked. No, she had not thought of that. She slumped against the wall between the two doors. Her arms were hanging limply at her side. There was no further need for telling her not to speak. How could she have spoken? He may have been moved by her despair, for he left Jeanne and took O in his arms, hugging her, calling her his love and his life, saying again and again that he loved her. The hand with which he was caressing her neck was moist with the odor of Jeanne. And so? The despair in whose tide she had been drowning slowly ebbed away. He loved her, yes, he did love her. He did have the right to take pleasure with Jeanne, or with the others; still he loved her. "I love you," she whispered in his ear, "I love you," so soft a whisper he could just barely hear.

"I love you."

It wasn't until he saw the sweetness flow back into her, and the brightness into her eyes, that he took leave of her, calm and contented.

Jeanne took O by the hand and drew her into the hallway. Once again their clogs clattered on the tiles and, once again, between the two doors, they found a valet sitting on a bench. He was dressed like Pierre, but it was not he. This one was tall, lean, and dark-haired. He rose and preceded them into an antechamber where, before a wrought-iron gate on either side of which hung a long green drape, two other valets were waiting, with several white russet-spotted hounds lying at their feet.

"That's the enclosure," Jeanne murmured. But the valet who had been walking ahead must have overheard her, for he turned around. O saw Jeanne grow deadly pale; she let go of her hand, let go of her dress which she had been holding with her other hand, and sunk to her knees on the black marble floor—for the antechamber was tiled in black marble. The two valets by the gate began to laugh. One of them came over to O, politely asking her to follow him. He opened a door opposite the one they had just come through, bowed, bade her pass. She heard the laughter and the sound of footsteps, then the door closed behind her. O never found out what happened, whether Jeanne had been punished for having spoken and, in being punished, how, or whether she had merely yielded to some caprice on the part of the valet, or if, in dropping to her knees, she had been obeying some regulation or invoking his mercy, or if she had succeeded. During O's first stay at the chateau, which lasted two weeks, she simply noticed that, absolute as the rule of silence might be, it was rare that in the course of frequent comings and goings or at meals one was not led into breaking it, especially during the day when only the valets were present. It was as if clothing somehow embolded one, affording a certain self- assurance which nakedness and nocturnal chains, and the presence of the masters, would destroy. She also noticed that while the slighest gesture in any way resembling an advance toward one of the masters appeared, quite naturally, inconceivable, one felt otherwise with the valets. The valets never issued orders, even though the politeness in which they couched their requests was just as implacable as an order. They were apparently under instruction to punish irregularities to which they alone were witness, and to punish them on the spot. Thus on three separate occasions, once in the hallway leading to the red wing and two other times in the refectory they had just begun to enter, O saw girls, caught talking, who were flung to the floor and lashed. It thus seemed that, despite what she had been told the first evening, one could be whipped during daylight hours, as if what went on with the valets did not count, as if these matters were left to their discretion.

Daylight gave their costume a curious and threatening look. Some of the valets wore black stockings, and, instead of the red jacket over the white ruffled shirt, a soft red silk shirt, gathered at the neck, wide in the sleeve, tight at the wrist. It was one of these valets who, on the eighth day, at noon, whip already in his hand, came over to near where

37

O was sitting and told a superb blonde named Madeleine, with breasts of milk and roses, to rise from her stool. A moment before that lovely girl had smiled at O and said something to her, but so rapidly that O had not understood. Even before he touched her shoulder she was already on her knees, her white hands fluttering under the black silk, drawing out the still drowsing sex, drawing it to her beautiful, half-opened mouth. That time she was not whipped. And since he was the only supervisor in the refectory at the time, and as he closed his eyes as he accepted the preferred caress, the other girls began to converse with their neighbors. There was, then, a way of bribing the valets. But what was the use? If there was any one regulation to which O had great trouble conforming, and to which she never really did conform, it was the one forbidding women to look into the faces of the men. Inasmuch as the same regulation applied to the valets, O felt herself in constant danger, given her devouring curiosity in connection with faces, and she was in fact whipped by both valets, not, it is true, every time they noticed her looking at their faces (for they took liberties in the interpretation of their instructions, and may have also placed a high enough value on the fascination they exerted not to deprive themselves, by too absolute and too effective application of the rules, of glances which never left their eyes and their mouths unless it were to descend to their sexes, their whips, and their hands, then begin, all over again), but doubtless only when they were moved by a desire to humiliate her. However cruelly they treated her, when indeed they had decided to treat her cruelly, she nevertheless always lacked the courage, or the cowardice, to fling herself at their knees; and although they did sometimes use her, she endured it, but she never solicited it. As for the rule of silence, it meant so little to her, except in the case of her lover, she never once disobeyed it, answering by means of gestures when some other girl, taking advantage of the occasional inattention of the guards, addressed her. This was generally at meals, which were served in the room she had been shown into when the tall valet escorting them had turned upon Jeanne. The walls were black, as were the flagstones underfoot, the long table of thick glass was black as well, and each girl had a round stool upholstered in black leather to sit on. One had to hoist one's skirt in order to take one's place, and, the smooth, cool leather, in contact with her thighs, made O remember that first moment when her lover had made her take off her stockings and panties and sit in that same way on the back seat of the car. Conversely, when later, after having left the chateau and being dressed like anyone else, but with her loins naked under her ordinary, everyday suit or dress, she always had to lift her slip and skirt whenever she sat down beside her lover, it was an overpowering memory of the chateau that came back to her: her breasts exposed and proffered by silken bodices, those hands and mouths to which nothing was denied, which could do as they pleased with everything, and that terrible silence. Nothing yet had been such comfort to her as the silence, unless it were the chains. The chains and the silence, which ought to have isolated her, smothered her, strangled her, had not. On the contrary, they'd been her deliverance, freed her from herself. What might have become of her had speech been accorded her and freedom granted her hands, had she had the freedom to choose when her lover prostituted her while he looked on? True, she had spoken under torture.

But does one designate as words those sounds which are only moans and screams? Besides, they often stilled her with gags. Beneath those stares, beneath the hands, beneath the sexes which defiled her, beneath those lashes which lacerated her, she sank, lost in the delirious absence from herself which gave her to love, and may have brought her close to death. She was anyone at all, no one, someone else, any of the other girls, being pried open and forced like her, girls whom she saw being pried open and forced—for she did see it, but even so she wasn't obliged to help do the opening or forcing.

On her second day, when not twenty-four hours had elapsed since her arrival at the chateau, she was taken after lunch to the library, and there her task was to serve coffee and tend the fire. Jeanne, whom the black-haired valet had brought back, went with her, and she was also accompanied by another girl, whose name was Monique. It was the same valet who escorted them there, and he remained in the room, standing by the pole to which O had been attached. The library was still deserted. Full-length French doors opened to the west, and the autumn sun, pursuing a slow arc through a vast, almost cloudless sky, spilled its rays on a commode, on which stood an enormous spray of chrysanthemums, smelling of sulphur-colored earth and dead leaves.

"Did Pierre mark you last night?" the valet inquired of O. She nodded.

"Then you ought not to hide it," he said. "Please roll up your dress."

He waited while she rolled up her dress behind, as Jeanne had done the evening before, and waited while Jeanne now helped her fasten her dress in place. Then he told her to light the fire. O's flanks to the height of her waist, her thighs, her slender legs were framed in the cascading folds of green silk and the white linen. The five welts had turned black. The kindling was ready beneath the logs, O had only branches to set a match to it. The kindling, of apple, caught at once, then the split oak logs, which burned with tall sparkling flames, were almost colorless in the strong afternoon light, but their odor was pungent. Another valet entered and placed a tray bearing the cups and the coffee on the console, from which the lamp had been cleared away, then withdrew. O moved near the console, Monique and Jeanne remained on either side of the fireplace.

It was then that two men entered, and now the first valet left. By his voice, O believed she was able to identify one of those who had forced her the previous evening, the one who had asked that her behind be made more accessible. O stole a glance at him while pouring coffee into the little black and gold cups which Monique distributed with sugar. So it would have been this frail blond young man with an English air about him. He was speaking again; she had no further doubt. The other was also blond, but short, heavy-set, and broad-faced. Both were seated in the big leather armchairs, their feet by the fender, smoking quietly and reading their newspapers, paying no more attention to the women than they would have if no women had been there. One now and again heard a soft rustle of newspaper, or the sound of coals falling on the hearth. Now and then O placed a new log on the fire. She was sitting on a cushion, on the floor near the wood-basket. Opposite her, Monique and Jeanne were also sitting on the floor. Their spread skirts overlapped. Monique's was dark red. All of a

41

sudden, but only after an hour passed, the blond youth summoned Jeanne, then Monique. He told them to bring the hassock (it was the hassock upon which O had been spread-eagled the evening before). Monique did not await further instructions: she kneeled down, bent over, squeezing her breasts against the surface of fur, and gripped the corners of the hassock with both hands. When the youth had Jeanne lift the red skirt, Monique lay completely still.

Jeanne had—and he gave her the order in the most brutal terms—to undo his garment and in both hands take that sword of flesh that had so cruelly pierced O, at least once. His member swelled and stiffened between shut palms, and O saw those same hands, Jeanne's little hands, spread Monique's thighs and, with little spasms which made him pant, the lad gradually penetrated her.

The other man, who had been looking on in silence, motioned for O to approach him, and, without diverting his attention from the spectacle, pushed her forward over one of the arms of his chair. Her raised skirt offered him a full view of the whole length of her behind; he seized her womb with his hand.

It was thus René found her when, a minute later, he opened the door.

"Don't let me disturb you, please," he said as he took his place on the cushion O had been occupying by the hearth before she had been summoned. He watched her closely and smiled each time the hand holding her, probing her, emerged and, working ever deeper, simultaneously explored both her apertures, which opened ever wider until at last she moaned, unable to restrain herself any longer.

Monique had long since gotten back on her feet, Jeanne

was tending the fire in O's place. René kissed her hand when she brought him a glass of whisky, which he sipped without taking his eyes off O.

The man who was still toying with her then spoke: "She's yours?"

"Yes," replied René.

"James is right, you know," said the other. "She's too tight. That's got to be remedied."

"Not too much though," said James.

"As you like," said René, rising. "You're a better judge of this than I." And he rang.

Thereafter, for eight days in succession, between nightfall, when her services in the library came to an end, and the hour in the evening, eight o'clock or ten ordinarily, when she was taken back to her cell, chained and naked under her red cape, O wore, inserted in her anus and held in place by three little chains attached to a leather belt circling her haunches, held, that is, in such a manner that the play of her internal muscles was unable to dislodge it, an ebonite rod fashioned in the shape of an upright male sex. One little chain following the fold between buttocks and thigh, and rose on either side of her belly's triangle so that, if anyone wished to, she could easily be penetrated there.

When René had rung, it was to have a servant bring the coffer, in one of whose compartments was an assortment of little chains and belts, and in another a selection of these shafts ranging from the thinnest to the thickest in size. They were all alike insofar as they flared at the base, to make certain that they'd not ride up and become lost in the body for, if this were to happen, the muscular ring might have contracted, whereas the object was for that ring to open and so stretch it. Thus she was spread wider a little

43

more every day, for James, who had her kneel down, or rather lie prone, and who looked on while Jeanne or Monique or whoever else it was who happened to be there introduced and secured the shaft he had picked out, each day a thicker one. At dinner, which the girls took together in the same refectory, but after they had bathed and were naked and made up, O would still be wearing it, and, because of the chains and the belt, everyone could see that she was wearing it. It was not removed except by Pierre, and then not until he came to chain her, whether to the wall for the night if no one were summoning her, or her hands behind her back if he was to take her back to the library. Rare were the nights when someone did not appear to make use of this passage which was in fact becoming so easy a thoroughfare, although still narrower than the other, needless to say. At the end of a week there was no further need of an instrument, and her lover told O he was happy now that she was doubly open, and, he said, he would see to it that she remained so. At the same time, he notified her that he was leaving, and that during the last seven days she was to spend at the chateau, before he returned to take her back to Paris, she would not see him.

"But I love you," he added, "I do love you. Don't forget me."

Forget him! Ah, how could she ever? He was the hand that blindfolded her, the whip the valet Pierre wielded, he was the chain above her bed and the stranger who ate her, and all the voices which uttered commands were his voice. Was she becoming weary? No. By dint of being outraged, it seemed as if she must have grown used to the outrages; by dint of being caressed, to caress, if not to the whip by dint of being whipped. A frightful surfeit of pain and joy, one

44

would have thought, should have edged her further and further along that gradually declining slope at whose lower depths are sleep and somnambulism. On the contrary. The corset which held her upright; the chains which kept her submissive; silence, her sanctuary—perhaps these had something to do with it, as was the constant spectacle of girls being pressed into use, and even when they were not being used, the spectacle of their always accessible bodies. Also, the spectacle and awareness of her own body. Daily and, as it were, ritualistically soiled by saliva and sperm, by sweat mingled with her own sweat, she sensed herself to be, literally, the vessel of impurity, the foul depths of which the Scriptures make mention. And yet those parts of her body which were the most continually offended, having become sensitive, seemed to her to have become, at the same time, more beautiful, and as though it were ennobled: her mouth closed on anonymous members, the tips of her breasts that hands were forever fondling, and between her wideflung thighs, the twin ways leading into her belly, paths wantonly trod. However astonishing it might seem, that she might be ennobled, that she might gain dignity from being prostituted, continued to amaze her. It illuminated her as if from within, and one could see a new calmness in her bearing, on her countenance the serenity and imperceptible inner smile one rather guesses at than perceives in the eyes of a recluse.

When René had informed her that he was leaving, night had already fallen. O was naked in her cell, waiting to be taken to the refectory. For his part, her lover was dressed as usual, in the suit he wore every day in town. When he took her in his arms the rough tweed of his coat chafed her nipples. He kissed her, lay down beside her on the bed, his

45

face to her face, and tenderly and slowly and gently took her, moving to and fro between the two passages offered to him, finally spilling himself into her mouth which he then kissed again.

"Before I go I'd like to have you whipped," he said, "and this time I ask your permission. Are you willing?"

She was willing.

"I love you," he repeated.

"Now ring for Pierre."

She rang. Pierre chained her hands above her head by the bed chain. When she was thus bound, her lover stepped up on the bed, kissed her, penetrated her again, told her that he loved her, then stepped back onto the floor and nodded to Pierre. He watched her writhe and struggle in vain; he listened to her moans develop into screams. When the tears had finished flowing, he dismissed Pierre. From somewhere deep within she found the strength to tell him again that she loved him. Then he kissed her drenched face, her gasping mouth, released her bonds, put her to bed, and left.

To say that from the moment her lover had left, O began to await his return would be an understatement. She turned into pure vigil, darkness in waiting expectation of light. During the day she was like a painted statue whose skin is warm and smooth, whose mouth is meek, and—it was only during this interval that she abided by the rule— whose eyes were always lowered. She made and cared for the fire, poured and passed around the coffee and liqueurs, lighted the cigarettes, arranged the flowers and folded the newspapers like a little girl busy in her parents' living room, so limpid with her exposed breast and her leather

46

collar, her tight bodice and her prisoner's bracelets, so demure, so yielding that it was enough for the men she served to order her to stand by them while they were violating another girl to make them want to violate her too; and that surely was why she was treated even worse than before. Had she sinned? Or had her lover, in leaving her, deliberately intended to make those to whom he lent her feel freer to dispose of her? At any rate, on the second day after his departure, as night fell, and after she had just undressed and was gazing at herself in the bathroom mirror, the marks that Pierre's crop had made on the front of her thighs being by now almost gone, Pierre entered. There were still two hours before dinner. He informed her that she would not dine in the common room, and bade her ready herself, pointing to the Turkish toilet in the corner where indeed he made her squat, as Jeanne warned her she would have to do in Pierre's presence. All the time she was there he stood contemplating her; she saw him in the mirrors, and saw herself incapable of holding back the water which escaped from her body. And still he waited, until she had bathed and made herself up. She was about to reach for her clogs and red cape when he stopped her and added, as he bound her hands behind her back, that she needn't bother, she should just wait there a moment. She sat down on a corner of the bed. Outside, gusts of cold wind were blowing, cold rain was falling, the poplar tree near the window swayed under the gale's attack. From time to time a pale wet leaf pasted itself against the window panes. The sky was pitch dark, as dark as the heart of night, even though the hour of seven had not yet struck, but autumn was moving on and the days were growing shorter.

47

Pierre returned. In his hand he carried the same blindfold they'd used that first night. He also had, clanking in his hand, a long chain similar to the one affixed to the wall. It appeared to O that he couldn't make up his mind which to put on her first, the chain or the blindfold. She watched the rain, not caring about his intentions or his hesitations, thinking only of what René had said, that he'd return, and that she had still five days and five nights to go, and that she didn't know where he was or if he was alone, and if he was not, who he could be with. But he would return.

Pierre had placed the chain on the bed and, without disturbing O's thoughts, fastened the black velvet blindfold over her eyes. It fitted snugly under the ridge of her brow and carefully followed the curve of her cheeks, making it impossible either to glance downward or even to raise her eyelids. Blessèd darkness like unto her own night, never had O welcomed it with such joy; oh blesssèd chains that bore her away from herself.

Pierre attached this new chain to the ring in her collar and invited her to accompany him. She stood up, felt herself being pulled along, and followed. Her bare feet froze on the icy tiles; she realized that she was walking down the red wing hallway, then the ground, as cold as before, became rough underfoot; she was walking on stones, sandstone, perhaps granite. Twice the valet brought her to a halt, twice she heard a key turn in a lock and a lock click as a door closed. "Be careful of the steps," said Pierre, and she descended a stairway; once she almost tripped. Pierre caught her around the waist. Before this, he had never touched her except to chain or beat her, but now here he was laying her upon the cold steps where, with her pinioned hands, she hung on as best she could to avoid slipping down, and he was playing with her breasts. His mouth was moving from one to the other, and as he pressed himself upon her, she felt his member gradually stiffen. It was only when he'd taken his pleasure with her that he helped her to her feet. Perspiring and trembling cold, she finally descended the last steps, then heard him open another door, through which she was led, immediately feeling a thick carpet under her feet. The chain was still being tugged, and then Pierre's hands released her hands and untied the blindfold; she was in a circular, vaulted room, quite small and low-ceilinged; the walls and arches were of unfaced stone, the joints in the masonry were visible. The chain attached to her collar was secured to an eye bolt set in the wall opposite the door, about a yard above the floor, leaving her free to move no more than two paces forward. Here there was neither a bed nor anything that might pass for one, there was no blanket, not a scrap of blanket, only three or four Moroccan-type cushions. They were out of her reach and clearly not meant for her. On the other hand, set in a niche from which shone the only light illuminating the room, lay a wooden tray; on it were water, fruit, and bread, and these were within her reach. The heat from the radiators, which had been installed at the base of, and recessed in, the walls, and which therefore formed a sort of burning plinth all the way around her, was nevertheless not enough to overcome the damp smell of mustiness and stone which is the odor of ancient prisons and, in old castles, of uninhabited dungeons. In this sultry, soundless twilight, O soon lost track of time. There was no longer any night or day, and never was the light turned off. Pierre or some other valet—it didn't matter which—replenished her supply of water, placed fruit and bread on the tray when none was left, and took her to bathe in a nearby dungeon. She never saw the men who entered, because, whenever they came, they were preceded by a valet who blindfolded her, and removed it only after they had gone. She also lost track of these visitors, how many there were, and neither her gently, blindly caressing hands nor her lips were ever able to identify who they touched. Sometimes there were several of them, most often they came alone, but every time, before she was approached, she was placed on her knees, her face to the wall, her collar fastened to the same bolt to which her chain was affixed, and whipped. She placed her palms flat against the wall and would press her face against the back of her hands, to avoid being scraped by the stone; but still it lacerated her knees and breasts. She also lost track of the whippings and of her screams, which were muffled by the vault. She waited. All of a sudden, time no longer stood still. In her velvet, anesthetic night she felt her chain being detached. She'd been waiting three months, three days, or ten days, or ten years. She felt herself being swathed in some heavy cloth, and someone taking her under the shoulders and under the legs; felt herself being lifted and carried away. She found herself in her cell again, lying beneath her black fur coverlet. It was early in the afternoon, her eyes were open, her hands were free, and there was René sitting beside her, caressing her hair.

"Come, get dressed," he said, "we're going."

She took one last bath, he brushed her hair, handed her her powder and lipstick. When she came back into her cell, her suit, her blouse, her slip, her stockings, her shoes were on the foot of the bed, her handbag and gloves, too. There was even the coat she put on over her suit when the weather began to get cold, and the square scarf she wore to protect her neck, but no garter belt or panties. She dressed slowly, rolling her stockings down to just above the knee, and she did not put on her jacket, for it was very warm in the cell. That was when the man who, that first evening, had explained what would be expected of her, came into the room. He unlocked the collar and the wristbands which had held her captive for two weeks. Was she freed of them? Or did she feel something was missing? She said nothing, hardly daring touch her fingers to her wrists, nor daring to raise them to her throat.

He then asked her to choose, from among all the identical rings he was presenting to her in a little wooden case, the one which would fit the ring finger of her left hand. They were curious iron rings, the inner surface of which was gold; the signet was massive, shaped like a knight's shield, convex and in gold niello bore a device consisting of a kind of three-spoked wheel, each spoke spiraling in toward the hub, like the solar wheel of the Celts. She tried the second one, then another, and, by forcing it a little, found that the second fitted her, though snugly. It felt heavy on her hand, and the gold gleamed almost secretly in the polished iron's dull gray. Why iron, and why gold? And the insignia she did not understand? But it wasn't possible to talk in this room, with its red draperies, with its chain still hanging over the bed, in this room where the black blanket, rumpled once again, lay on the floor, where the valet Pierre might enter, would surely enter, absurd in his operetta costume, in the dull light of November.

She was mistaken. Pierre did not enter. René had her put on her suit jacket and her long gloves that reached up over the bottoms of the sleeves. He took her scarf, her bag, and

51

folded her coat over his arm. The heels of her shoes made less noise on the hallway floor than her clogs had, the doors were shut, the antechamber empty. O held her lover's hand. The stranger who accompanied them opened the grilled gate, which Jeanne had said was the enclosure gate and which neither valets nor dogs were guarding now. He raised one of the green velvet curtains and ushered them both through. The curtains fell back again. They heard the grilled gate click shut. They were alone in another antechamber, which looked onto the garden. They now had only to descend a short flight of steps, and there in the driveway was the car, which O recognized.

She sat down next to her lover who was at the wheel, and they started off. When they'd gone through the main gate, which was wide open, and driven a hundred yards or so, he stopped and kissed her. It was on the outskirts of a peaceful little village they came to a moment or two later. O saw the signpost. On it was painted: Roissy.

2

Sir Stephen

*T*he Ile Saint-Louis apartment where O lived was on the top story of an old building on a southern quay overlooking the Seine. The rooms were mansarded, spacious and low, and the two of them that were on the facade side opened onto a balcony set between the sloping sections of the roof. One of them was O's bedroom; the other—where full-length bookcases framed the fireplace—served as a living room, a study, and could, if necessary, be used as a second bedroom. There was a broad divan facing the two windows, and a large antique table in front of the fireplace. If her dinner guests were too numerous, they would eat here instead of in the small dining room, decorated in dark green serge, which looked out on the court. Another room, also looking out on the court, was René's, where he kept his clothes and would dress in the morning. They shared the yellow bathroom and the tiny yellow kitchen. O had a cleaning woman come in every day. The rooms overlooking the court were tiled in red—the tiles were the antique, hexagonal tiles one still finds on stair treads and landings from the second floor up in old Parisian hotels. Seeing them again gave O a shock and made her heart beat faster: they were the same as the tiles in the Roissy hallways. Her bedroom was small, the pink and black chintz curtains were drawn, the fire glowed behind the screen, the bed was made, the covers turned back.

"You didn't have a nylon nightgown," said René, "so I bought you one." True: there, unfolded on the side of the bed where O slept, was a white nylon nightgown, pleated, tailored, fine, like one of the garments that appear on Egyptian statuettes. It was so sheer it was nearly transparent. O tried it on: she tied the thin belt around her waist to conceal the series of elastics inside. O noticed that the nightgown was so sheer her flesh turned it a pale pink.

Everything in the room—except for the curtains and headboard panel overlaid with the same material and the two little armchairs upholstered in the same chintz—was white: the walls, the fringe round the mahogany four-poster bed, the bearskin rug on the floor. Wearing her new white nightgown, O sat down by the fire to listen to her lover.

He told her that, to begin with, she mustn't think of herself now as free. Except in one sense: she was free to stop loving him and to leave him immediately. But if she did love him, then she was no longer free. She listened to him without saying a word, thinking how happy she was that he wanted to prove to himself, no matter how, that she belonged to him; but also thinking that there was a naïveté in his failing to realize that the degree to which he possessed her lay beyond any proof. Perhaps, though, he did realize it, and wanted only to emphasize it? Perhaps he enjoyed emphasizing it to her? She gazed into the fire while he talked; but he, unwilling or not daring to meet her gaze, was looking elsewhere. He was on his feet, pacing to and fro. Suddenly he said that, before anything else, in order for her to hear what he was saying he wanted her to unlock her knees and unfold her arms, for she was sitting with her knees together and her arms folded around them. So she drew up her skirt and, kneeling, or rather sitting back on her heels, in the posture of the Carmelites or Japanese women, she waited. Except that, with her knees spread, she felt, between her parted thighs, the faint prickling of the white bearskin fur. No, he insisted, that wouldn't do, she wasn't opening her legs wide enough. The word "open" and the expression "open your legs," when uttered by her lover, would acquire in her mind such overtones of restiveness and of power that she never heard them without a kind of inward prostration, of sacred submission, as if they had emanated from a god, not from him. So she remained perfectly still, her hands, palms turned upward, resting beside her knees, the folds of her nightgown lying in a quiet circle around her.

What her lover wanted of her was very simple: that she be constantly and immediately accessible. It wasn't enough for him to know that she was: every obstacle to her accessibility had to be eliminated, by her carriage and manner in the first place, and, in the second place, by the clothing she wore, she would signify her accessibility to the initiated, to those who knew. That, he continued, involved two things. The first she already knew, for on the evening of her arrival at the chateau it had been made clear to her that she was never to cross her legs, as she was to keep her lips open at all times. All this, she probably thought, meant very little (she did in fact think exactly that), but she was wrong: on the contrary, she would discover that conformance to this discipline would require a constant effort of attention,

57

which would forever remind her, when the two of them, and perhaps certain others, were together, even though in the midst of the most everyday occupations and while among those who did not share the secret, of what her condition really was. As for her clothing, it was up to her to choose it and, if need be, to devise a costume which would render unnecessary that half-undressing he had submitted her to in the car while taking her to Roissy: tomorrow she would go through her closets and bureau drawers and sort out every last garter-belt and pair of panties, which she would hand over to him: he would likewise take all the brassieres, like the one whose shoulder-straps he'd had to cut in order to remove it from her, all the slips she had whose upper part covered her breasts, all her blouses and dresses which didn't open in front, any of her skirts which were too narrow to be raised instantly, with a quick motion. She'd have other brassieres, other blouses and other dresses made. Between now and then was she to go to her corset-maker with her breasts naked under her blouse or sweater? Yes, he replied, that was how she would go to her corset-maker, her breasts naked under her blouse or sweater. If anyone were to notice and comment she could explain it any way she liked, or make no explanation at all; either way, that was her affair and no concern of his. Now, as far as the rest of what he had to tell her, he preferred to wait a few days and when, the next time she sat down to listen to him, he wanted her to be dressed properly. In the little drawer of her writing desk she'd find all the money she would need. When he had finished speaking, she murmured: "I love you," without the slightest gesture or expression. It was he who added some wood to the fire, lit the pink opaline bedside lamp. Then he told O to get into bed and wait for him, that he was going to sleep with her. When he returned, O reached over to turn off the lamp: it was her left hand, and the last thing she saw before darkness engulfed everything was the somber glitter of her ring. Propped up on one elbow, lying on one hip, she then touched the switch; at that same moment her lover's low voice summoned her by name; she went to him, he laid his hand on her womb and drew her to him.

The next day, O was in the dining room, alone in her dressing gown, having just finished lunch—René had left early and wasn't due back until evening to take her to dinner—when the telephone rang. The phone was in her room, on the bedside table by the lamp. O sat on the floor and picked up the receiver. It was René. Had the cleaning woman left? Yes, she'd gone just a moment ago, after serving her lunch, and she wasn't due back until the following morning.

"Have you started to go through your things?" René asked.

"I was just about to," she replied, "but I got up very late and didn't finish my bath till noon."

"Are you dressed?"

"No, I'm in my nightgown and bathrobe."

"Set the receiver down—no, don't hang up, set it on the bed. Take off your nightgown and bathrobe."

O obeyed, so startled that the receiver slipped off the bed and fell onto the white rug. Hastily, fearing the connection had been cut off, she snatched it up, said: "Hello."

No, they had not been cut off.

"Are you naked?" René asked.

"Yes," she said. "Where are you calling from?"

He didn't reply.

"You're still wearing your ring?"

She was still wearing it.

Then he told her to stay as she was until he returned and, thus undressed, to put the things she was throwing away into a suitcase. Then he hung up.

It was after one o'clock, the weather was clear. A patch of sunlight fell on the rug, lighting the white nightgown and the corduroy bathrobe, pale green, like the hulls of fresh almonds, which O had let slip to the floor after she had taken them off.

She picked them up and started toward the bathroom to hang them up in a closet. On the way, she passed a three-sided mirror, formed by one panel mounted on a door and two others, one straight ahead and one on the right, at a turn in the hall. She saw her reflection: she was naked except for the leather clogs, the same color as her bathrobe—not much darker than the clogs she had worn at Roissy—and the ring. She was no longer wearing a collar or leather wristbands, and she was alone, her sole spectator. And yet she had never felt so totally subject to a foreign will, never so a slave, and so happy to be one.

When she bent over to open a drawer, she saw her breasts sway softly. It took her almost two hours to lay out on the bed the clothes she was supposed to put into the suitcase. First, the panties; there was no problem there, they all went into a little pile by the bedpost. The same for the brassieres; they all had to go, for they all had a strap and fastened at the side. But she noted that the same model could perfectly well be made with the catch in the front, just under the cleavage between her breasts. Out went the garter belts too, but she hesitated about getting rid of the rose satin brocade corset which laced up in the back and

60

which so closely resembled the bodice she'd worn at Roissy. So she put it aside on the dresser. René would decide. He'd also decide about the sweaters which, without exception, went on over the head and were tight at the neck, hence couldn't be opened. But they could be pulled up from the waist by anyone wanting access to her breasts. On the other hand, there was no doubt about the full-length slips, they were in a pile on the bed. In the bureau drawer there was still one half-slip, black faille hemmed with fine Valencienne lace at the bottom, made to be worn beneath a pleated sun skirt of black wool, shear enough to be transparent. She'd need other half-slips, light-colored and short. She also realized that she would have to give up wearing sheath dresses, but that she might be able to get the same effect from a dress that buttoned all the way down in front, and it might be possible to have a built-in slip made which would unbutton at the same time as the dress. As for the petticoats, there wasn't likely to be any problem, nor with the dresses, but what in the world would her dressmaker say about the underclothes? She'd tell her she wanted a detachable lining because she was sensitive to the cold. Come to think of it, she was sensitive to the cold, and suddenly she wondered how, with the light clothing she would be wearing, she would bear the cold in the winter.

Finally, when she'd finished the job, and from her wardrobe salvaged only those blouses that buttoned in front, her black pleated skirt, her coats of course, and the suit she'd worn back from Roissy, she went to make some tea. She turned up the thermostat in the kitchen; the cleaning woman hadn't remembered to fill the firewood basket, and O knew that her lover liked to find her in the living

61

room by the fire when he came home in the evening. She filled the basket from the pile of wood in the hallway closet, carried it into the living room, and started a fire. Thus did she wait for him, curled up in a big easy chair, the tea tray next to her. But this time, as he had ordered, she awaited him naked.

The first difficulty O encountered was at work. Difficulty? Not quite. Rather, she met with astonishment. O worked in the fashion department of a photography agency, which meant that, in the studio where they posed hour after hour, she took the pictures of the most exotic and prettiest girls whom the fashion designers had selected to model their gowns.

They were astonished, or at least surprised, that O had taken her vacation this late in the autumn and, in so doing, had been absent during the very period when professional activity was at its height, when new styles were about to be created. But they were even more surprised at the change that had taken place in her. At first glance, you couldn't tell in just what way, but you sensed there had been some sort of change, and the more you looked at her the surer you were. She stood and walked straighter, her gaze was clearer, but what was most striking was her perfection when she was in repose and, when she moved, how measured were her movements.

She'd always dressed conservatively, as women do when their work resembles men's, but so cleverly that sobriety seemed quite right for her. The other girls, who constituted her subjects, and who were constantly concerned with O's clothing and adornments as part of their profession, were quick to detect what other, less-observant eyes might not

62

have noticed. Sweaters worn next to the skin, which softly outlined her breasts—René had ended up permitting her to wear sweaters—pleated skirts which, when she turned, swirled so readily, these took on the quality of a discreet uniform.

"Very little-girl-like," said a blond, green-eyed model with high Slavic cheekbones and an olive complexion, "but you're wrong not to wear a garter belt. You're going to ruin your legs wearing garters all the time." The comment was occasioned by O, who had sat down one day somewhat hastily in the model's presence, and without paying much attention, on the arm of a heavy leather chair, and her skirt had, for a moment hiked itself up. The tall girl had caught a flash of naked thigh above the rolled stocking which stopped just above the knee.

O had seen her smile, so curiously that, at that very instant, she'd wondered what the girl had been thinking, or perhaps understood. She pulled her stockings up tight, first one stocking, then the other (it wasn't as easy keeping them tight that way as it was when they ended at mid-thigh and when garters held them in place), and replied, as if to justify herself:

"It's practical."

"Practical for what?" Jacqueline asked.

"I don't like garter belts," O answered.

But Jacqueline wasn't listening to her; her eyes were fixed on the iron ring.

During the next few days O made some fifty photographs of Jacqueline. They were like none she had ever taken before. Perhaps she had never had such a model before. In any case, she had never before been able to extract such meaning and feeling from a face or a body. Yet all she was trying to do was to highlight the silks, the furs, the laces, with the fairytale loveliness, the suddenly awakened surprise that swept over Jacqueline no matter what she was wearing, the simplest blouse or the most elegant mink. Her hair was cut short, it was thick and blond, slightly curly, and, as they were readying the shot, she'd cock her head ever so slightly toward her left shoulder, leaning her cheek against the upturned collar of her fur, if she was wearing fur. O caught her once that way, smiling and sweet, her hair faintly blown as though by some gentle breeze, and her smooth, hard cheekbones nestled against the mink, as gray and delicate as fresh firewood ash. Her lips were slightly parted, her eyes half-closed. Under the cool brilliance of glossy paper, one would have thought this the picture of some blissful victim of a drowning, she was pale, so very pale. From the negative O had made a high-contrast print. She had taken another photograph of Jacqueline, even more stunning than the first: this one was back-lighted, her shoulders bare, her finely shaped head and delicately featured face enveloped in a large-mesh black veil that was surmounted by absurd-looking egret feathers wafting upward in a wispy crown of smoke. She was wearing a voluminous gown of heavy brocade, red silk, such as brides wore in the Middle Ages, a gown that fell to within inches of the floor, flaring at the hips, tight at the waist, and whose armature accentuated her breasts. Nobody ever wore such dresses anymore, it was what the designers called a gala-gown. The very spike-heeled sandals were also of red silk. And all the while Jacqueline was there before O in this gown and sandals, and that veil which was like a suggestion of a mask, in her mind O completed the image, modified it according to an inner prototype: a shade of this,

64

a shade of that—that waist drawn in a little more tightly, the breasts raised a little more sharply—and it was the Roissy dress, the same dress Jeanne had been wearing, the same smooth, cascading silk one seizes by the handful and raises when one is told to . . . . And, yes, Jacqueline was holding it, lifting it as she stepped down from the platform where she had been posing for a quarter of an hour. It was the same rustling, the same crackling like dry leaves. Nobody ever wears such dresses any longer? Oh, but there are still some who do. Jacqueline also was wearing a golden choker around her neck, two golden bracelets on her wrists. O caught herself imagining that she would be lovelier with a collar and with leather bracelets. And then she did something she'd never done before: she followed Jacqueline into the large dressing room, adjacent to the studio, where the models dressed and made up and where they left their clothes and make-up when they left. She leaned against the doorjamb, her eyes fixed on the dressing table mirror before which Jacqueline, still wearing her gown, had just sat down. The mirror was so tall—it covered the whole back wall of the room, and the dressing table was an ordinary slab of black glass—that O could see both Jacqueline's and her own image, and also the image of the costume assistant who was detaching the egret plumes and removing the tulle veil. Jacqueline undid her choker herself, her arms lifted like two swans' necks; a trace of sweat glistened in her armpits, which were shaven (why shaven? what a pity, thought O, she is so fair), and O could smell the sharp, pungent plant-like odor, and wondered what perfume Jacqueline ought to wear—what perfume they would make Jacqueline wear. Then Jacqueline undid her bracelets, posed them on the glass slab where, for a brief moment, they made a noise like chains clanking. She was so fair haired that her skin was darker that her hair, beige, like fine sand after the tide has gone out. On the photo, the red silk would come out black. At that moment, the thick eyelashes Jacqueline put on only to satisfy the requirements of her job lifted, and in the mirror O caught a glance so direct, so steady, that, although she was unable to remove her own gaze from Jacqueline, she sensed a warm glow in her cheeks. That was all, just one glance.

"I beg your pardon," Jacqueline said, "I have to undress."

"Excuse me," O murmured, and closed the door.

The next day she took home the prints made the day before, not knowing whether she did or did not want to show them to her lover, with whom she was dining out that evening. While making up at the dressing table in her room, she gazed at them and would now and then pause to touch the photo and trace the line of an eyebrow, the suggestion of a smile. But when she heard the sound of a key in the front door, she slipped the prints into the drawer.

For two weeks O had been entirely outfitted and ready for use, and she was not getting used to it. Then, coming home one evening from the studio, she found a note from her lover asking her to be ready at eight to join him and a friend for dinner. A car would be sent to pick her up, the chauffeur would come and ring at her door. In a postscript he asked her to wear her fur jacket, dress entirely in black (entirely was underlined), and take care to make up and perfume herself the way she had at Roissy.

It was already six o'clock. Entirely in black, and for dinner—and it was mid-December, cold outside, that meant black silk stockings, black gloves, the pleated skirt, her heavy-knit sweater with spangles or her crepe page-boy jacket. She thought it had better be the page-boy jacket. It was padded and quilted in large squares, reinforced and stiff from collar to waist, like the tight-fitting doublets men wore in the sixteenth century, and the reason it molded her bust so perfectly was because the brassiere was built into it. It was lined with the same faille, and the slit tails reached down to her hips. It was black everywhere except for the large gold hooks, which looked like those on children's snow boots, opening and closing with a clicking sound made by the large flat clasps.

After she had laid her costume out on the bed and, at the foot of the bed, set her black suede shoes with platform soles and spiked-heels, O thought it the strangest thing in the world to find herself in her own bathroom, free and alone after her bath, meticulously making herself up and perfuming herself, as she had done at Roissy. Her cosmetics weren't the same as the ones used there, however. In the drawer of her dressing table she found some face rouge, which she never used, which managed to accentuate the halo around her nipples. It was one of those rouges one barely sees when applying it, but whose color deepens later on. At first she thought she'd put on too much, so she wiped off a little with alcohol—it didn't wipe off easily— and began again: she achieved a dark pink at the tips of her breasts. In vain she sought to rouge the lips hidden by the fleece of her belly, but the rouge left no apparent trace. Among the various lipsticks she had in the same drawer, she finally found one of those kissproof types she didn't like to use because they were too dry and too hard to remove. But for present purposes the kissproof variety worked fine. She did her hair, freshened her face, then perfumed herself.

René had given her, in an atomizer which expelled a thick spray, a perfume whose name she didn't know, but which had an odor of dry wood and wild plants. The mist melted on her skin, flowed over the hair under her arms and at her belly, forming tiny droplets.

At Roissy O had learned not to be in a hurry: she perfumed herself three times, each time letting the perfume dry. First she put on her stockings and her high heels, then the half-slip and the skirt, then the jacket. She put on her gloves and took her bag. In her bag were her compact, her lipsticks, a comb, her key, and a thousand francs. Wearing her gloves, she took her fur coat from the armoire, glanced at the time on her bedside clock: it was quarter to eight. She sat down on the edge of the bed and, her eyes riveted to the dial of the alarm clock, in perfect repose waited for the sound of the doorbell. When she heard it and rose to leave, before turning out the light, she glanced at the dressing table mirror and saw her reflected gaze: bold, gentle, and docile.

When she opened the door to the little Italian restaurant before which the car had stopped, the first person she saw was René, who was at the bar. He smiled tenderly, took her hand and, turning toward a sort of grizzled athlete, introduced her in English to Sir Stephan H. O was offered a stool between the two men, and as she was about to sit down, René whispered to her to be careful not to wrinkle her dress. He helped her slide her skirt out from under the edge of the stool, and she felt the cold leather pressed against her skin, while the cold metal rim pressed against the lower part of her womb itself, for she dared not sit all the way down at first, fearing that, if she did, she might yield to the temptation to cross her legs. Her skirt hung down all around her. Her right heel was hooked on one of the rungs of the stool, the tip of her left foot touched the floor. The Englishman, who without saying a word had simply made an imperceptible bow, had not taken his eyes off her; she noticed him study her knees, her hands, finally her lips— but study them so calmly, and with an attention so precise and so sure of itself, that O felt herself being weighed and measured as the instrument she knew very well she was, and it was as though under the pressure of his gaze and, so to speak, in spite of herself, that she removed her gloves: she knew that he would speak as soon as her hands were bare—because her hands were unusual, resembling those of a youth rather than those of a woman, and because, on the third finger of her left hand, she was wearing the iron ring with the triple gold spiral. But no. He didn't say anything, he smiled: he had seen the ring. René was drinking his second martini and O the grapefruit juice René had ordered for her. He said that unless O were otherwise disposed, she would do him the kindness of concurring in their view that it might be better to go downstairs to eat, for the dining room below was smaller and less noisy than this one which, on the ground floor, was hardly separated from the bar.

"Certainly," said O, who had already picked up her bag and gloves, which she had placed on the bar.

Sir Stephen helped her down from the stool, offering her his right hand, in which she laid hers, he finally addressed her directly, to observe that such hands were made for irons, so admirably did iron become her. But as he said it in English there was a faint ambiguity in the words, and one might be in doubt whether he was referring only to the metal or, perhaps more specifically, to iron chains.

The room downstairs was a simple cellar, whitewashed but airy and pleasant, with, it turned out, only four tables, one of which was occupied by guests who were finishing their meal. On the walls were frescos, a gastronomic map of Italy done in soft ice-cream colors: vanilla, raspberry, pistachio. Looking at the frescos, O decided to ask for an ice-cream dessert, with almonds and whipped cream. For she felt in a happy, light-hearted mood; under the table René's knee touched hers, and when he spoke, she knew he was talking to her alone. He too was gazing at her lips. Her request for ice cream was granted, but they said no when she asked for coffee. Sir Stephan proposed that O and René join him for coffee at his home. All three had dined very lightly, sparingly, and O remarked to herself that, if the men had drunk very little, she had been allowed to drink even less: half a liter of chianti for the three of them. And they had eaten quickly too: it was only a few minutes after nine.

"I dismissed the chauffeur for the evening," said Sir Stephen. "René, will you drive?" The simplest thing would be to go straight to my place."

René took the wheel, O sat next to him, Sir Stephen next to her. The automobile was a large Buick, with ample space for three in the front seat.

After the Alma round-about, the Cours de la Reine was clearly visible through the leafless branches of the trees, and the place de la Concorde was sparkling and dry. Overhead those dark clouds promised snow, which couldn't make up its mind to fall. O heard a click and felt warm air rising along her legs: Sir Stephen had turned on the heater. René followed the Right Bank a little while longer, the took the Pont Royal Bridge to the Left Bank: between the bridges' stone arches the Seine looked as frozen as stone, and just as

70

black. O thought of hematites, which are black. When she'd been fifteen, her best friend, who'd been thirty and with whom she'd been in love, had worn a ring with a hematite set in a cluster of tiny diamonds. O had always wanted a necklace of those black stones, without diamonds, a tight-fitting necklace, even a choker. But the collars they gave her now—no, they didn't give them—would she have exchanged them for the hematite necklace of her adolescent dreams? Once again she saw the poor, unkempt room Marion had taken her to, behind the Turbigo intersection, and remembered how she, not Marion, had untied her two large schoolgirl's braids after Marion had undressed her and had her lie down on the iron bed. When she was being caressed, Marion was beautiful, and it's true that eyes can look like stars; Marion's had resembled twinkling blue stars.

René parked the car. O didn't recognize this little street, one of those cross streets between the rue de l'Université and the rue de Lille.

Sir Stephen's apartment was at the far end of a courtyard, in a wing of an old private mansion, and the rooms were laid out in a line, one opening into the next. The room farthest from the entrance was the largest and the most restful, furnished in dark English mahogany and pale silk, striped yellow and gray.

"I won't ask you to tend the fire," Sir Stephen said to O. "But this couch is for you. Please, sit down. René will see to the coffee. I would like you simply to hear me out."

The broad damascus-covered couch was set perpendicular to the fireplace, facing windows overlooking the garden, and away from other windows, on the far side of the room, which overlooked the courtyard. O removed her fur and draped it over the back of the couch. When she turned around, she saw that her lover and Sir Stephen were both standing, waiting for her to comply with Sir Stephen's invitation. She put her bag near the fur and unbuttoned her gloves. When, when, she wondered, would she ever find the one rapid and unobtrusive gesture which would enable her to lift her skirts at the same time she sat down so that no one would notice, the gesture which would allow her to forget her nakedness, her submission? It would not at any rate be so long as René and this stranger stared at her in silence, as they were now doing. She finally yielded. Sir Stephen stirred the fire, René suddenly passed behind the couch and, seizing O's neck and hair, drew her head against the back of the couch and kissed her on the mouth, kissed her so long and so profoundly that she lost her breath, gasped, and felt a burning, melting sensation in her belly. He released her only to say that he loved her; then he immediately took her again. O's hands, the palms turned helplessly upward, lay silently on the black dress spread like a corolla around her. Sir Stephen had approached and when René finally let her go and she opened her eyes, it was the gray, unflinching gaze of the Englishman they encountered.

Bewildered, and dizzy with joy, she was nevertheless able to see that he was looking at her admiringly, and that he desired her. Who could have resisted her moist, half-opened mouth, her full lips, her white neck flung back against the black collar of her page-boy jacket, her eyes wide-open and bright, her steady gaze? But Sir Stephen's only gesture was to caress her eyebrows and then her lips, softly, with the tip of his finger. Then he took a place opposite her, on the other side of the fireplace, and when René had also seated himself in an armchair, Sir Stephen began to speak.

"I don't believe René has ever spoken to you of his family," he said. "You may perhaps know, however, that before she married his father, René's mother was married to an Englishman who had a son by his first marriage. I am that son, I was brought up by René's mother until she left my father. So, strictly speaking, I am not related to René, and yet, in a way we are brothers. René loves you, of that I am sure. I would have known it even had he not told me, even if he had not made a move. It's enough to see the way he looks at you. I also know that you are one of those who have been to Roissy, and I dare say you will be going back there. Theoretically, I have the right to do as I like with you; the ring you are wearing gives me that right as it does to anyone else who knows what it means. But the mere exercise of my right is one thing; what we want from you is far more serious. I say 'we' because, as you observe, René isn't saying anything: he prefers that I address you in both his behalf and mine. If we are brothers, I am the elder, he being ten years younger than I. Between us there also exists a freedom so absolute and of such long standing that what belongs to me has always been his, and vice-versa. Will you consent to common ownership? I very much hope you will, and I ask the question because your acquiescence will require much more on your part than your submission, which we take for granted. We should like to move beyond that stage. Before replying, consider that I am merely, and cannot be other than, another form of your lover: a somewhat more formidable master, I expect, than the men to whom you were surrendered at Roissy; for I'll constantly be there. And besides," Sir Stephen concluded, uttering this final phrase in English, "I have a fondness for habits and rites."

His calm, self-assured voice pierced an absolute silence.

Even the flames in the fireplace danced soundlessly. O was as though frozen to the couch, like a butterfly impaled upon a pin, a long pin of words and glances which penetrated the middle of her body and nailed her naked and attentive loins to the warm silk. She no longer seemed mistress of her breasts, her hands, the nape of her neck. But of one thing she was certain: the object of those habits and that ritual was going to be the possession of (among other parts of her body) the long thighs hidden beneath her black skirt that were already open.

The two men were sitting across from her. René was smoking, but had lit one of those black-hooded lamps which counteract smoke, and the air in the room, purified by the wood fire, had the cool smell of night.

"Will you answer me now?" Sir Stephen inquired. "Or would you like me to tell you more?"

"If you give your consent," René put it, "I myself will explain Sir Stephen's preferences to you."

"My demands," Sir Stephen corrected.

Consent, O was thinking, was not the difficult part, and it was then she realized that neither of the men had for one moment anticipated the possibility of her not consenting; nor in fact had she. Speaking, saying anything—that was the hardest part. Her lips were on fire, her mouth was dry, the saliva wasn't there anymore, an anguish composed of fear and desire constricted her throat, and her hands, which she had recovered control of, were cold and clammy. If only she could have but closed her eyes. But no, two gazes stalked hers; she could not elude them, nor did she want to. They drew her back toward what she thought she had left behind for a long time, perhaps forever, at Roissy. For since her return René had always taken her by means of caresses,

74

and the symbol declaring that she belonged to whoever knew its secret had simply been without any consequences: either she had not encountered anyone who knew the secret, or, if she had, they had not betrayed the fact—the one person she could possibly suspect was Jacqueline (and if Jacqueline had been at Roissy, why didn't she too have a ring? And, furthermore, if Jacqueline did know the secret, what rights over O did that knowledge confer on her?). Did she have to move in order to speak? But she couldn't move of her own accord—an order would have brought her to her feet immediately, but this time what they wanted from her was not blind obedience to an order, it was that she voluntarily acknowledge herself as a slave and surrender herself as such. That is what they called her consent. She recalled that she had never said anything to René except "I love you" and "I'm yours." Today it seemed as if they wanted to have her speak, and specifically agree to what, until now, only her silence had accepted.

In the end she straightened up and, as if what she had to say was smothering her, unfastened the upper clasps of her tunic, baring herself to the cleavage between her breasts. Then she stood up. Her knees and hands were trembling. "I am yours," she told René at last. "I'll be whatever you want me to be."

"No," he said, "you're to be ours. Repeat after me: `I belong to both of you. I will be whatever both of you want me to be.'"

Sir Stephen's hard gray eyes remained fixed upon her, as were René's; under those gazes she foundered, slowly repeating the phrases her lover dictated to her, dutifully substituting the pronouns from the second person into the first: it was like a grammar lesson: "You acknowledge my and Sir Stephen's right . . ." said René, and, in as clear a voice as she could muster, O responded: "I acknowledge your and Sir Stephen's right . . ." The right to dispose of her body as they saw fit, in whatever place or manner they pleased, the right to keep her in chains, the right to flog her as a slave is flogged or as is one sentenced to punishment, for whatever cause or simply for their pleasure, the right to ignore her pleas and cries, if they were to make her cry out.

"I believe," said René, "that it is at this point Sir Stephen would like me to step in, assuming you and I both agree, and brief you on what he expects of you."

O listened to her lover, and the words he had addressed to her at Roissy returned to her: they were almost identical to these. But then, at Roissy, she had, while listening to those words, been snuggled up against him, had been shielded by a feeling of the improbable, had been able to hide behind the feeling that she was undergoing some other existence or perhaps that she didn't exist at all. Dream or nightmare, the prison setting, the party costumes, the people in masks, all this had denied reality, transported her out of the realm of her everyday life and transported her far away to a place where time ceased to exist. At Roissy, she had felt herself to be as one is at night, lost in a dream one has dreamed before and which begins all over again: sure that the dream exists, sure that it will end, you would like to have it end because you are afraid of being unable to bear it, and you would like it to continue because you are afraid of not finding out how it will end. Well, here was the end, right here, just where you would have least expected it, and in the most unexpected of all imaginable forms (assuming, of course, as she now said to herself, that this was indeed the end and that there wasn't some other end hidden behind it, or perhaps still a third ending hidden behind the second one). What distinguished this end was the way it made recollection topple into the present; and the way, also that what had formerly only been reality in a closed circle, in a private domain, was all of a sudden about to contaminate all the habits and circumstances of her daily life, both upon her and within her, was no longer to be content with outward signs—naked loins, laced-up bodices, the iron ring—but to require the thoroughgoing accomplishment of an act.

It was true that René had never whipped her, and the only difference between the period before he had taken her to Roissy and the period since their return, was that he now did with her mouth and behind what in the past he had only done (and was continuing to do) with her womb. At Roissy, she had never known whether the beatings she had so regularly received had been, even once, administered by him (when there had been occasion for doubt about the matter, when she was blindfolded or those dealing with her masked), but she tended to doubt it. In all likelihood, his pleasure was so great simply in watching her bound and helpless body's vain struggles and in hearing her screams that, in order not to miss anything of the spectacle, he would doubtless have refused to take a more active part in it, since it would have distracted his attention. So that what he was now saying amounted to a form of confession; she heard him say—so sweetly, so tenderly, without stirring in the large overstuffed chair in which he was reclining, with his legs crossed, how happy he was to hand her over, how happy he was that she was handing herself over, to Sir Stephen, to his commands and wishes. Should Sir Stephen wish her to spend the night with him, or merely an hour, or desire her to accompany him outside of Paris or to some play or concert or restaurant in Paris, he would telephone her and send his car for her—unless René himself came to pick her up. Today, now, it was for her to speak. Did she consent? But she could find no words.

This willful assent they were suddenly asking her to express, was the agreement to surrender herself, to say yes, in advance, to everything to which she very surely did want to say yes but to which her body was saying no, at least insofar as the whip was concerned. As for the rest, if she were to be honest with herself she would have to admit that she was too shaken by the desire she read in Sir Stephen's eyes, a feeling too intense, to deceive herself, and as she was trembling, and perhaps precisely because she was trembling, she knew she was waiting with greater impatience than he for the moment when he would place his hands, and perhaps his lips, on her. Doubtless—obviously—it was her role to hasten that moment. Whatever her violent desire, whatever courage she may have had, she suddenly felt herself grow weak, and as she was on the point of replying she slipped to the floor, her dress in a pool around her, and, in the silence, she heard Sir Stephen's leaden voice opine that fear was also becoming to her. The remark was directed not to her, but to René. O had the impression that he was holding himself in check, refraining from advancing on her, and she regretted that self-control. However, she was not looking at him, her eyes were fixed on René. She was terrified that he might detect in hers what he might consider a betrayal. And yet it wasn't a betrayal; for if she were to have weighed her desire to be had by Sir Stephen against her belonging to René, she would not have hesitated a second; she was allowing herself to succumb to this desire only because René had permitted her to, and, to a certain extent, made her to understand that he was ordering her to. Yet there was a lingering doubt in her mind: might René not be irritated to see her acquiesce so quickly and so easily? The least sign from him would have effaced that doubt in a trice. But he made no sign, confining himself to ask her, for the third time, for an answer. She stammered: "I agree to whatever the two of you desire," then lowered her eyes to her hands which were waiting, unclasped beside her knees; then added, in a murmur: "I'd like to know if I shall be whipped . . . ."

There was a long pause; during which, twenty times over, she regretted her question. Then at last Sir Stephen said, in a slow drawl: "Occasionally."

Next, O heard a match being struck and the tinkling of glasses: both men were probably pouring themselves another round of whiskey. René was leaving O to her own devices. René was silent.

"Even if I consent to it now," she said, "even if I give my promise now, I won't be able to bear it."

"You are simply being asked to submit to it, and if you scream, if you beg for mercy, to consent, ahead of time, that it will be in vain," Sir Stephen continued.

"Oh, have pity on me!" said O, "not again, no more of that," for Sir Stephen had risen to his feet. So had René; he was leaning over, gripping her shoulders.

"Answer," he said. "Do you consent?"

Finally she said that she did consent. He gently helped her up and, sitting down, he had her kneel on the floor alongside him, facing the couch upon which her outstretched arms, head, and bosom were resting. Her eyes were closed.

It was then that a memory came back to her: several years before she had seen a curious print showing a woman kneeling, as she was, before an armchair. The floor of the room was tiled, a child and a puppy were playing in one corner. The woman's skirts were raised, and a man standing nearby was brandishing a handful of switches, preparing to beat her. All the figures were wearing late sixteenth-century costumes and the print bore a title which had struck her as revolting: Family Discipline.

One of René's hands held her wrists in a vicelike grip while with the other he was raising her skirts, raising them so high that she felt the muslin lining brush her cheek. He was caressing her flanks, her loins, drawing Sir Stephen's attention to the twin dimples there, and the softness of the furrows between her thighs. He then placed that same hand upon her waist, squeezed it to accentuate her buttocks, and commanded her to open her knees further. Without a word, she did as she was told. The liberties René was taking with her body, his enthusiastic commentary upon it, Sir Stephen's replies, the coarseness of the language the two men were employing, overwhelmed her with shame, as violent as it was unexpected, so that the desire she had for Sir Stephen vanished, and she began to long for the lash as a deliverance, for pain and screams as a justification. But Sir Stephen's hands opened her womb, forced apart her buttocks, penetrated, released her, seized her again, caressed her until she moaned. She was humiliated, undone, and ashamed she had moaned.

"I leave you to Sir Stephen," René then said. "Stay as you are, he'll send you back when he wishes." How many times had she remained like this at Roissy, on her knees, waiting for whoever might want her? But at Roissy she had always

80

been constrained by the wristbands locking her hands together, the lucky captive upon whom everything was inflicted, of whom nothing was asked. Here it was of her own free will that she remained half-naked: the same will that would bring her body to subjection. Her promise bound her inexorably, as had leather bracelets and chains. Was it only her promise that bound her? And however humiliated she was, or rather because she was humiliated, was there not a sweetness in being valued because of her humiliation, of her docile willingness to bow down, her obedience to open herself?

René had gone, Sir Stephen having escorted him to the door. She waited by herself, motionless, feeling more exposed in the solitude, more prostituted in the waiting than she had ever felt when the two men had been there in the room. The gray-and-yellow striped silk covering of the couch was smooth beneath her cheek; through her nylon stockings she felt the thick carpet under her knees, and upon the full length of her leg the heat emanating from the fire to which Sir Stephen had added three logs, which were now burning noisily. An antique clock on a commode ticked so quietly that only now was she able to make out the sound, in the stillness. O listened attentively, fully aware of the immense absurdity, in this well-appointed, civilized drawing room, of being in such a position. From the further side of the draw curtains came the drowsy rumbling of Paris after midnight. In tomorrow morning's daylight, would she recognize the place where she had laid her head on the sofa cushion? Would she ever, in broad daylight, be able to return to this same drawing room, to be treated in the same way again?

Sir Stephen had still not returned; and O, who had so

submissively awaited the strangers at Roissy to take their pleasure, was now struggling with the thought that in a minute, in ten, he would once again lay his hands on her. But it didn't turn out quite the way she'd expected.

She heard him open the door, shut it, and cross the room. He remained standing for awhile with his back to the fire, contemplating O; then, in a very low voice, bade her get up from where she was kneeling, and sit down. She obeyed, surprised and almost embarrassed. Courteously, he brought her a glass of whiskey and a cigarette, both of which she declined. She then noticed that he was in a dressing gown, a simple robe of gray homespun—the same tone of gray as his hair. His hands were long and thin; his nails, trimmed short and flat, were very white. He intercepted O's gaze, she blushed; these were the same hands that had laid hold of her body, which now she dreaded, now desired. But he didn't come near her.

"I should like to have you undress, entirely," he said. "But first, without getting up, unfasten your jacket."

O unfastened the large gilt clasps and, slipping the close-fitting jacket down over her shoulders, she put it at the far end of the couch, where her fur, her bag, and her gloves were.

"Caress your nipples, caress them very lightly," said Sir Stephen, who added: "You must use a darker rouge. What you are using is too light." Stupefied, O teased her nipples with her fingertips until she felt them harden and rise; she hid them with the palms of her hands.

"No," said Sir Stephen, "don't."

She removed her hands and lay back on the couch: her breasts were heavy for so slender a torso, and parting, rose gently toward her armpits. The nape of her neck rested

82

against the back of the sofa, her hands resting on either side of her hips. What was keeping Sir Stephen from bringing his mouth to hers? Why did he not bring his hand toward the nipples he had wished to see stiffen and which she felt quiver with each breath she took? But he had come near, he was sitting on the arm at the end of the couch, but he was not touching her. He was smoking. His hand twitched—O never knew whether that movement was voluntary or not—and in so doing it caused a bit of hot ash to fall between her breasts. She had the feeling he wanted to insult her by his disdain, his silence, his detachment. Yet he had desired her a short while before, he still did now, she could tell by the straining bulge under his robe's soft material. Oh, then let him take her, even if it were only to wound her! She detested her own desire, she detested Sir Stephen for the self-control he was displaying. She wanted him to love her, there, the truth was out: wanted him to be impatient to touch her lips, to penetrate her body, to lay her waste, but not maintain this calm, not impose this terrible restraint on his pleasure. At Roissy it had made not the slightest difference to her whether those who used her had felt anything at all: they were the instruments by means of whom her lover derived pleasure from her, by means of whom she became what he wanted her to be, as smooth and cool as a pebble in a brook. Their hands had been his hands, their orders his orders. But not now, not here. René had turned her over to Sir Stephen, but it was plain that he wanted to share her with him, not to obtain more from her, but to share with Sir Stephen what at the present time he cherished most, as in the days, when they had been younger, they had shared a journey together, a boat, a horse. And today this sharing derived its meaning much

83

more from René's relation to Sir Stephen than from René's to her. What each of the two was looking for in her would be the mark of the other, the trace of the other's passage. A little while ago, when she had been kneeling half-naked against René, and when Sir Stephen had opened her legs with both hands, René had explained how O's buttocks had become so distended, and why he had been delighted to see it so prepared: he had at the time thought of how much Sir Stephen would enjoy having the path he preferred always available; René had even gone on to say that if Sir Stephen liked, he, René, would leave its use entirely to him.

"Why, gladly," Sir Stephen had said, but he had remarked that, stretched though it did appear to have been, there was still some danger that he might tear O.

"O belongs to you," René had replied immediately, "O will be happy to be torn."

And he had bent toward her and kissed her hands.

The mere idea that René could thus imagine depriving himself of some part of her had stunned O. She saw it as an indication that she meant less to her lover than did Sir Stephen. And too, although he had so often told her that what he loved about her was the object he had made of her, the absolute disposition of her he enjoyed, the freedom that was his to do with her what he wished, as one is free to dispose of a piece of furniture which one takes as much, and sometimes more, pleasure in giving away than in keeping for oneself, she realized now that she had not entirely believed him.

She saw yet another sign of what one could hardly call deference toward Sir Stephen, in the fact that René, who so passionately loved to see her beneath the bodies or blows of others besides himself, who with such devoted tenderness, with such constant gratitude, would watch her mouth open to emit moans of pleasure or screams, watch her eyes close tight over tears, had left her after making sure, in exposing her, in opening her secret parts the way one opens the mouth of a horse and exhibits the teeth to show that the animal is young enough, that Sir Stephen found her pretty enough, or at least suitable, for his own purposes and was willing to accept her. This behavior, however, insulting and outrageous, changed nothing with respect to O's love for René. She considered herself fortunate to know that she was important enough in his eyes to enable him to find pleasure in offending her, as believers thank God for having humbled them. But in Sir Stephen she divined a will of ice and iron which desire was powerless to deflect from its purpose and before which, until now, as enticing and as submissive as she might be, she counted for absolutely nothing. Otherwise why would she have experienced such fear? The scourge tucked in the Roissy valet's belts, the almost constantly worn chains, had seemed less dreadful to her than the equanimity in the gaze Sir Stephen trained on her breasts, on breasts he did not deign to touch. Upon her little shoulders and slender torso she could feel their weight; smooth and full, she knew how fragile they were. She could not make them stop trembling; to do that she would have had to stop breathing. To hope that this fragility would disarm Sir Stephen was futile, and she knew very well that, on the contrary, her proffered sweetness, her helplessness cried out for wounds as much as caresses, fingernails as much as lips. She had a momentary illusion: Sir Stephen's right hand, the one holding his cigarette, grazed her nipples, his middle finger grazed their tips, which responded by stiffening. Was this, for Sir Stephen,

85

some sort of game and no more, some sort of verification, such as one might use to test the excellence and proper functioning of a mechanism? O was in no doubt about the answer.

Still perched on the arm of the sofa, Sir Stephen then told her to get rid of her skirt. The clasps didn't readily unhook under O's moist fingers, it took two tries before she succeeded in getting out of the black faille half-slip under her skirt.

When she was at length completely naked, her patent-leather high-heeled slippers and her black nylon stockings, which were rolled down to just above her knee, emphasizing the slender lines of her legs and the whiteness of her thighs, Sir Stephen, who had also risen, seized her womb with the spread fingers of one hand and pushed her toward the couch. He made her kneel down, her back against the sofa, and to make her lean more of her weight against her shoulders, he had her spread her thighs slightly. This brought her waist forward, away from the sofa. Her hands lay by her ankles. Her sex gaped wide. Above her still proffered breasts was her exposed throat, for she had flung her head back.

She didn't dare look at Sir Stephen's face, but, from the corner of her eye, she saw his hands untie the belt of his dressing gown. When he had approached her, was standing straddling her, when he had seized her by the nape of the neck, he drove himself into her mouth. It wasn't the caress of her lips along the length of his member he was seeking, but rather the depths of her throat. He thrust, thrust again, probed for a long time, and O felt the suffocating gag of flesh swell and harden, and still he thrust, and the repeated hammering brought tears to her eyes. The better to invade her, Sir Stephen had knelt on the sofa, one knee of either side of O's face, and there were times when his buttocks rested on O's breasts, and she felt her womb, useless and scorned, burning. Despite the great length of time he spent in her mouth, Sir Stephen did not bring his pleasure to a climax, but finally withdrew from her in silence, stood up, without closing his dressing gown. "You are easy, O," he said. "You love René, but you are easy. I wonder whether René realizes it. Is he aware that you yearn for every one of the men who desire you? Is he aware that in sending you to Roissy or in surrendering you to others he is simply providing you with ready-made alibis for your own easy virtue?"

"I love René," O replied.

"You love René, but you also yearn for others. Me for example," Sir Stephen said.

Yes, she did desire him, but if René were to hear it, would he change? She didn't know; all she could do was keep still and lower her eyes: to have gazed at Sir Stephen would have been tantamount to a confession.

Then Sir Stephen approached and, taking her by the shoulders, made her lie down on the rug: she found herself on her back, her legs drawn up, her knees flexed. Sir Stephen had seated himself on the same spot on the sofa where, a moment ago, she had been leaning; he seized her right knee and pulled her to him. As she was facing the fireplace, the nearby fire shed an intense light upon the two well-opened furrows of her womb and buttocks. Without letting go of her, Sir Stephen curtly ordered her to caress herself, but not to close her legs. Startled, she obediently stretched her right hand toward her sex and her fingers encountered, between the parted fleece, the already burning morsel of flesh placed above where the fragile lips came together.

She touched that flesh, then abruptly removed her hand and stammered:

"I can't."

And she actually could not. She had never caressed herself except furtively in the warmth and obscurity of her own bed, when she had slept alone; and never had she pursued her pleasure to a climax. She'd gone to sleep and sometimes the climax would come later, in a dream, and she had waked, disappointed that it had been simultaneously so strong and so fleeting.

Sir Stephen's stare was insistent, compelling. She could not bear it and, repeating her "I can't," she shut her eyes. For she saw it again, and couldn't get it out of her mind: every time she saw it she had the same sickening sensation she'd had when she had actually witnessed it when she was fifteen years old: Marion slumped down in a leather armchair in a hotel room; Marion, one leg flung over an arm of the chair and her hand half-hanging over the other arm: caressing herself, and moaning, in front of O. Marion had told her that she'd once caressed herself that way in her office, at a time when she thought there was no one else there; and the boss had suddenly walked in and caught her in the act.

O remembered Marion's office: a bare room, pale green walls, north light filtering through dusty windows.

There was one chair in the room, intended for visitors and it was opposite the table.

"Did you run away?" O had asked. "No," Marion had replied, "he asked me to go ahead and start again, but he locked the door and made me take off my panties and he'd moved the chair over by the window."

O had been overwhelmed with admiration for what she'd considered Marion's courage, and with horror, and had shyly but stubbornly refused to caress herself in front of Marion, and had sworn that she'd never caress herself in front of anyone. Marion had laughed and said: "You'll see. Wait till your lover asks you to."

René had never asked her to. Would she have done it if had he asked? Of course she would, but she would also have been terrified that she might see in René's eyes the same look of disgust she had felt while watching Marion. Which was absurd. And since it was Sir Stephen, that was even more absurd; what difference did it make to her if Sir Stephen were disgusted? But no, she couldn't. For the third time, she murmured:

"I can't." Low as was the voice in which she uttered those two words, he heard it, released her, rose, tied his robe shut, and ordered O to get up.

"Am I to take that for obedience?" he asked.

Then he caught her two wrists in his left hand, and, with his right hand, slapped her hard. She staggered and would have fallen had he not held her up.

"Kneel down, I have something to say to you," he said. "I'm afraid René has prepared you very poorly."

"I always obey René," she stammered.

"You are confusing love and obedience. You're going to obey me without loving me and without my loving you."

Whereupon she felt a storm of revolt rise in her, silently denying the words she had heard, denying the promises of submission and slavery she'd given, denying her own consent, her own desire, her nakedness, her sweat, her trembling legs, the circles under her eyes. She clenched her teeth in rage and fought when, having moved behind her, he bent

89

her over till her elbows and forehead touched the floor, raised her haunches, and drove himself into her, tearing her as René had said he would.

The first time she did not scream. He went to work more brutally, and this time she screamed. And every time he withdrew, then plunged in again, she screamed, as much out of revolt as from pain, and he knew it. She also knew too, and knowing it was the measure of her defeat—that she was beaten and that it pleased him to force her to scream. When he was done and, after having pulled her to her feet, was on the point of dismissing her, he advised her that what he had spilled in her was going to seep out gradually, to trickle out mixed with the blood from her wounded flesh, that this wound would go on burning her so long as her buttocks refused to accommodate themselves to him, and that he was going to go on tearing it until it did. René had reserved to Sir Stephen this way of using her, and he fully intended to take full advantage of his brother's generosity. He reminded her that she'd consented to be René's slave and his too, and it seemed to him that she knew what she had agreed to; no, in all likelihood she had not yet. But by the time he'd taught her it would be too late for her to escape.

Listening to him, O told herself that, with the determined resistance she intended to put up, it would also perhaps be too late for him to avoid becoming enamored of her and end up loving her a little. For all her inner resistance, and the timid refusal she'd dared to display, had but one object: in some slight degree, she wanted to exist for Sir Stephen in the way she existed for René, and she wanted him to feel something more than desire for her. Not that she was in love with him, but because she clearly saw that

René loved Sir Stephen with the passion young boys have for older boys, and because she sensed that, if need be and to satisfy Sir Stephen, he was prepared to sacrifice her to any of Sir Stephen's slightest whims, in an effort to please him. A powerful intuition told her that René would for Sir Stephen's example and that if Sir Stephen were to exhibit contempt for her, René, no matter how much he loved her, would be contaminated by that contempt as he had never been before or even dreamed of being influenced by the attitudes of the men at Roissy. The point was that at Roissy, as far as she was concerned, René had been the master, and the attitude of everyone to whom he gave her had depended upon his attitude. Here, René was no longer the master. On the contrary, Sir Stephen was the master of René, whether or not René fully realized it; that is, René admired him, was striving to imitate him, to rival him, which is why he shared everything with him and why he had given him O: this time, she had been given with no strings attached. In the future, René's love for her would probably align itself with how much or how little Sir Stephen judged she was worth bothering with, and only so long as René loved her himself. Thus, until Sir Stephen began to love her, he would be her master and, regardless of what René might suppose, her only master in the strictest sense of the master-slave relationship. She expected no pity from him; but was there absolutely no hope of wresting some affection from him?

Sprawled back in the big armchair by the fire René had occupied before departing, Sir Stephen had left her standing naked in front of him, with instructions to await his further orders. She had waited without saying a word. Then he had got to his feet and told her to follow him. Still naked, except for her high- heeled shoes and black stockings, she followed him up the stairway which began at the ground-floor landing, until they reached a room so small that there was space in it for only one bed, a dressing table, and, between the bed and the window, a single chair. This little room communicated with a larger one, Sir Stephen's, and both shared a bathroom.

O washed and wiped herself dry—spots of pink remained on the towel—removed her shoes and stockings, and crawled in between the cold sheets. The window curtains were open, but the night outside was black.

Before closing the door between their rooms, Sir Stephen approached her—she was already in bed—and kissed her fingertips, as he'd done when she'd got down off the bar stool in the restaurant and when he'd complimented her on her iron ring. Thus he had been able to thrust his hands and his sex into her, to ravage her behind and her mouth, but he had only deigned to touch his lips to her fingertips. O wept, and only fell asleep toward dawn.

Shortly before noon the next day, O was taken home by Sir Stephen's chauffeur. She had woken up at ten, an elderly black woman had brought her a cup of coffee, prepared her a bath and given her her clothing, except for the fur, the gloves and the handbag, which she found on the drawing room sofa when she went downstairs. The drawing room was empty, the venetian blinds were raised, and the curtains were open. Through the window opposite the sofa, she could see a narrow garden, as green as an aquarium and planted in nothing but ivy, holly, and spindle hedges.

As she was putting on her coat, the servant informed her that Sir Stephen had gone out but had left a message: the woman handed her an envelope on which only her initials were written. The white sheet of paper inside bore two lines: "René telephoned to say he would pick you up at six at your studio"; by the way of signature, only an S; and finally, at the bottom of the page, a postscript: "The riding crop is for your next visit."

O looked around the room: on the table between the two armchairs, where Sir Stephen and René had been sitting the night before, there was, lying beside a bowl of yellow roses, a long, slender leather riding crop. The servant was waiting for her at the door; O dropped the letter in her bag and left.

So René had phoned Sir Stephen, and not her. Once home, having taken off her clothes and lunched in her dressing gown, she still had plenty of time to freshen her make-up, comb her hair and change clothes before setting out for the studio, where she was due at three. The telephone didn't ring, René didn't call her. Why? What had Sir Stephen told him? What had they said about her? She remembered the words in which they had so casually discussed, from the point of view of their own physical requirements, the advantages her body offered. Maybe it was just that she wasn't used to this sort of vocabulary, but for these English terms the only French equivalents she could find were base and contemptible. True, she had been as handled and fondled as a prostitute in any brothel, so why shouldn't she be called a whore? "I love you, René, I love you," she repeated, whispering to him in the solitude of her room, "I love you, do whatever you want with me, but don't leave me, for God's sake, don't leave me."

What pity is there for those who wait? They are so immediately recognizable: by their gentleness, their falsely attentive stare—attentive, yes, but to something else than what they seem to be looking at—by their absent-minded-ness, are they known. In the studio she had a little plump red-headed model who was modeling hats for her, she didn't know the girl; for three hours O was that absent-minded person lured into forgetfulness by anguish, by her desire for time to pass more quickly.

Over a red silk blouse and petticoat she'd put on a plaid skirt and a short suede jacket. The bright red blouse showing through her half-open jacket made her pale face paler, and the little red-head had said she looked like a femme fatale. "Fatal to whom?" O wondered.

Two years earlier, before she had met René and fallen in love with him, she would have sworn: "Fatal for Sir Stephen" and have added: "He's going to know it, too." But her love for René and René's love for her had robbed her of every weapon, and instead of bringing her new proofs of her power, had deprived her of those she'd possessed till then. Once she'd been indifferent and fickle, had amused herself tempting the boys who were in love with her, she'd tease them with a word, with a gesture, but never yield an inch, and when later she did yield, she'd only do it once, just for fun and to reward them for having played the game, but also to inflame them further, and to make a passion she didn't share even more cruel. She'd been sure they had loved her. One of them had tried to commit suicide; when he'd come home cured, from the hospital where he'd been taken, she went to see him at his place, took off all her clothes, and, forbidding him to lay a finger on her, had lain down on his couch. White with desire and pain, he'd stared at her for two hours, silent and petrified by the promise he had made. She had never wanted to see him again. It wasn't that she didn't take seriously the desire she aroused

94

in him. She took it seriously enough, for she understood it, or thought she understood it, since she experienced (or so she thought), a similar desire for her girlfriends or for unknown young women. Some of them yielded to her—those she'd then enticed into some discreet hotel with narrow corridors and paper-thin walls—while others had backed off in horror from her proposals. But what she took to be desire didn't go a great deal further than the thirst for conquest, and neither her tough-guy manners, or the fact that she'd had several lovers—if one could call them lovers—nor her hardness, nor even her courage had been of the least use to her when she'd met René. In the space of a week she became acquainted with fear, but also with certainty, also with anguish, but also with happiness. René threw himself at her like a pirate springing on a captive, and she reveled in her captivity, feeling on her wrists, her ankles, all over her limbs and far down into her heart's and body's secret recesses, bonds subtler, more invisible than the finest hair, stronger than the cables with which the Lilliputians made Gulliver prisoner, bonds her lover would tighten or loosen with a glance. She was no longer free? Yes, thank God, she was no longer free! But she was light as a nymph goddess, swift as a fish of the deep, forever doomed to happiness. Doomed because those powerful strands, those thin cables whose ends René held in his hand, were the only lines by which the current of life could reach her.

That was so true that when René slackened his grip upon her—or when she imagined he had—when he seemed distant, or when he retreated into what O took to be indifference, or when he let some time go by without seeing her or answering her letters, and when she thought he no longer cared or was about to cease loving her, everything came to a halt in her, she languished, she smothered. Green grass turned black, day ceased to be day, night to be night, becoming instead infernal machines which made light alternate with darkness specifically in order to torture her. Cool water made her nauseous. She felt like a pillar of salt, a statue of ash, bitter, useless and damned, like the salt statues of Gomorrah. For she was guilty, a sinner. Those who love God and whom God abandons in the dark of the night, are guilty, they are sinners because they are abandoned. What sins have they committed? They search for them in their memory. She would seek for them in hers. She would find nothing beyond silly little self-indulgences which derived more from her acts of kindness or personality than from anything she had done, such as trifling with the desires in men other than René, to whom she paid attention only because of the happiness René's love gave her, only because her happiness at belonging to him, filled her with joy, and, abandoned as she was to him, that submission made her vulnerable, irresponsible, and all her inconsequential acts—but what acts? For she could only reproach herself with thoughts and fleeting temptations. Yet, one thing was certain: she was guilty, and, without wanting to, René was punishing her for a sin he knew nothing about (for it was entirely an inner sin), but which Sir Stephen had detected instantly: her wantonness.

O was happy René had her whipped and prostituted, because her impassioned submissions would give her lover proof that she belonged to him, and also because the pain and the shame of the lash, and the outrage inflicted on her by those who forced her to pleasure when they took her, and at the same time delighted in their own pleasure without being the least bit concerned about hers seemed to her to be the very absolution of her sins. There had been appalling couplings, hands on her breasts that had been intolerable insults, mouths which had inhaled her lips and tongue like so many soft, repulsive leeches, and tongues and sexes, bestial and vicious and clinging, which, caressing her closed mouth, both her openings below, which she had done her best to squeeze tight, had stiffened her with revolt, turned her so permanently stiff that it had been all the whip could do to unbend her, but the blows had finally opened her, with an abominable, disgusting servility. And what if, despite all that, Sir Stephen were right? What if she actually derived pleasure from her debasement? If so, then the baser, the viler she was, the more merciful was René to consent to make O the instrument of his pleasure.

When she was a child she had read a text written in red letters on the white wall of the room she'd lived in for two months in Wales: a passage from the Bible, such as Protestants often inscribe in their houses: "It is a terrible thing to fall into the hands of the living God." No, she said to herself now, no, that isn't true. What is terrible is to be rejected by the hands of the living God. Every time René postponed the moment he was to meet her, as he had done that day—for it was after six; it was after six-thirty—O was brought to the verge of madness and despair, in vain. Madness for naught, despair, there was no truth anymore. René arrived, he was there, he hadn't changed, he loved her, but he'd been held up by a staff meeting or had some additional work to attend to, he hadn't had a moment to call her to say he'd be late. O, in a flash, emerged from her airless chamber, and yet each of these accesses of terror would leave behind a premonition, something that would remain in the depth of her being, a warning of woe: for René had neglected or forgotten to call her up when the reason for his tardiness was a round of golf or a bridge game, or perhaps some other face had held him up, for he loved O, but he was free and he was sure of her, and casual, so casual. A day of death and ashes, a day among so many other days, might not a day come that would justify the madness, a day when the gas chamber's door would not reopen? Ah! Let the miracle last, let me still be touched by grace, oh, René, don't leave me! O didn't look further, and refused to look further, than every day's tomorrow and every tomorrow's tomorrow, she refused to look beyond this week into next, and beyond next week into the one after that. And for her every night with René was a night that would last forever.

René finally arrived at seven, so delighted to see her again that he kissed her in front of the electrician who was fixing one of her floodlights, right in front of the little red-headed model who was coming out of the dressing room, and right in front of Jacqueline, whom no one was expecting, and who suddenly entered the studio hard on the heels of the other model. "What a charming sight," Jacqueline said to O.

"I was just passing by and wanted to ask you to let me see those shots we took. But I guess this isn't the moment, I'll be on my way."

"Please, Mademoiselle! don't go," said René, without letting go of O, whom he was holding by the waist. "Mademoiselle! Don't go, really."

O introduced them: Jacqueline, René; René, Jacqueline.

Piqued, the red-headed model had vanished into the dressing room, the electrician was doing his best to look busy. O gazed at Jacqueline and sensed René following her gaze. Jacqueline was in a ski outfit, the sort only movie stars who don't ski wear. Her black sweater accentuated her small, widely-spaced breasts, her tapered black pants did the same for her winter-sports-girl long legs. Everything about her suggested snow: the bluish sheen of her gray seal-skin jacket, was snow in shadow; the wintery glint of her hair and eyelashes, snow in the sunshine. She was wearing a dark red lipstick, almost purple, and when she smiled, and her eyes settled on O, O told herself that no one could possibly resist the desire to drink of that clear green, moving water under the frosty lashes, nor to rip off that sweater to lay hands on her small breasts. There it was: René was no sooner by her side than, full of the self-assurance created by his presence, she recovered her taste for others, for herself and for the world.

They left the studio together, all three. Rue Royale, the snow, which had been falling in huge flakes for two hours, was still coming down, but now in little flakes, no longer soft, but hard, and they stung the face. The salt scattered on the sidewalks crunched underfoot and melted the snow, and O felt the icy breath of melting snow rise up beneath her skirt and fasten on her naked thighs.

O had a fairly clear idea what she was looking for in the young woman she pursued. It wasn't that she was trying to give herself the impression of competing with men, nor was she trying, by means of masculine behavior, to compensate for some female inferiority she didn't feel in the slightest. True, she'd once, at twenty, when she was courting one of her prettiest friends, surprised herself doffing her beret to say hello, standing back to allow her friend to go first, and offering a hand to help her out of a taxi. Similarly, she wouldn't stand for not paying her share of the check when she and a female friend went for some tea in a pastry shop. She would kiss her hand and her mouth too, if possible right there in the middle of the street. But all that simply amounted to carefully calculated behavior, stemming from a certain childishness than to her conviction. On the other hand, the strong liking she had for the sweetness of very sweetly painted lips yielding to hers, for the enameled or pearly flash of eyes that half-close in the subdued light of sofas at five o'clock in the afternoon, when the curtains have been drawn and the lamp on the fireplace mantel lit, for voices that say: "Again, oh for God's sake, again"; for the well-nigh ineffaceable marine odor that clung to her fingers: that penchant was strong, it was real, and it was profound.

Strong too was the pleasure she derived from hunting. Probably not the hunt itself, however amusing or exciting it could be, but the perfect freedom she felt when she hunted. She controlled the game, and she alone (which, with a man, she never did unless it were on the sly). She took the initiative, she initiated the conversations, made the rendezvous; she instigated the kisses, even to the point where she preferred not to receive but always to give the first kiss, and from the time she began to have lovers, she would almost never allow the girl she was caressing to caress her. The greater her desire to see a friend naked before her eyes, the less she found any reason to take off her own clothes. Often she made up excuses to avoid undressing: said she was cold, that it was the wrong time of the month. In fact, few were the women in whom she failed to find some element of beauty; she remembered the time when, just after having left school, she had wanted to seduce an ugly, disagreeable ill-natured little girl simply because she had a wonderful mop of blond hair which, in unevenly cut strands, created a chiaroscuro upon a somewhat faded but fine-grained, smooth, but quite lusterless skin. But the little girl had driven her away, and if pleasure had ever at any time lit her ungrateful face, it had not been out of thanks to O. For O passionately loved to see a face become transformed by that mist which renders faces so smooth and so youthful; a timeless youthfulness which is not a return to childhood but which causes the lips to become fuller, makes the eyes larger, the way makeup does, and puts a sparkle in the iris. In this, admiration's role was more important than pride, for it wasn't her handiwork that moved O: at Roissy, she had experienced the same uneasiness in the presence of a face of a girl being possessed by someone she did not know. Nakedness, the body's abandon, had overwhelmed her, and it seemed to her that her girlfriends had bestowed on her a gift for which she could never make a like return when they simply agreed to display themselves naked in a closed room. For vacation nudity, in the sunshine on the beach, affected her not at all—not at all because it was public, but because by being public and by not being absolute it was, to some degree, protected. The beauty of other women, which with unfailing generosity she was inclined to find superior to her own, nonetheless did reassure her regarding her own beauty, in which she saw (when one of her stray glances caught her own reflection in some mirror), like a reflection of theirs. The power she acknowledged her girlfriends had over her was at the same time the guarantee of her own power over men. And what she asked of women (and didn't return, or ever so little), she was happy, and found entirely natural, that men should be desperate to demand of her. Thus was she simultaneously the accomplice of both women and men, and stood only to gain with both. There were times when the game wasn't always easy. That O was in love with Jacqueline, no more and no less in love with her than she'd been with a lot of others, and admitting the phrase "in love" was the correct one (it was also a strong one), there was no doubt. But why did she go to such lengths to hide it?

When the buds opened on the poplar trees and when daylight, lingering now along the quays, allowed lovers time to sit on the benches in the public gardens after work, she thought she'd mustered up enough courage to confront Jacqueline. In winter, Jacqueline had looked too triumphant in her cool furs, too iridescent, untouchable, inaccessible. And she knew it. Springtime put her in suits and flat heels and sweaters, and gave her the appearance, with her short-cut straight hair, of those insolent sixteen-year-olds at the Lycée whom O, then a student herself, had seized by the wrists and silently drawn into cloakrooms and thrust up against the massed coats. The coats would fall from their hangers. O would burst out laughing. They used to wear uniform blouses of raw cotton, their embroidered initials in red cotton on their breast pockets. Three years later, and three kilometers away, Jacqueline had worn the same blouses in some other lycée. So O learned that by chance one day when Jacqueline put aside the dress she'd been modeling and, with a sigh, remarked that if they had clothes as pretty as these at school, they would have been a lot happier. Or if they had been allowed to wear the jumper they gave you, but without anything underneath.

"What do you mean, without anything?" O asked. "Without a dress, of course," Jacqueline replied. At which O began to blush. She couldn't get used to being naked under

102

her dress, and any equivocal remark seemed to her an allusion to her condition. In vain she repeated to herself that one is always naked under one's clothes. No, she felt as naked as the Italian woman of Verona who, to save her besieged city, went out to offer herself to the enemy chief: naked under a coat which one simply needed to open a crack. It also seemed to her that her nakedness was an atonement for something, like the Italian woman, but for what? Jacqueline was sure of herself, she had nothing to atone for; she didn't need to be reassured, all she needed was a mirror. O gazed at her humbly, thinking that the only thing one could offer her were magnolias because their thick, ripe petals turn softly into bister when they fade, or perhaps camellias, because their waxen whiteness is sometimes infused with a pink glow. As winter retreated, the faint tan which gilded Jacqueline's skin disappeared with the memory of snow. In a little while, only camellias would do. But O dreaded being laughed at, with these melodramatic flowers. One day she brought a large bouquet of blue hyacinths, whose heady odor is like that of tuberoses: oily, strong, cloying, and precisely the odor camellias ought to have but don't. Jacqueline, who'd been wearing a pink lipstick for the last two weeks, buried her pert little nose in the stiff, warmly humid flowers. "Are they for me?" she asked, as do those women who are used to receiving gifts from everyone.

She said thank you, then asked if René was going to come by for O. "Yes," said O, "he's coming by later." He's going to come, she repeated to herself, and it will be for him that Jacqueline, falsely still, falsely silent, will briefly raise her ice-water eyes which never look one straight in the face. No one would ever need to teach this woman any-

103

thing: neither to be silent, not how to arch her head halfway back. O was dying to seize a handful of the too-blond hair at the nape of her neck, to force that docile head all the way back, to trace the line of those eyebrows with at least her finger. But René would want to do that, too.

She knew full well why, once afraid of nothing, she had become so shy, why she had desired Jacqueline for two months without betraying that desire by so much as a word or a gesture, and was lying to herself to explain this self-restraint. It wasn't true that Jacqueline was intangible. The obstacle was not with Jacqueline; it lay deep within O herself, and was so firmly implanted she'd never had to deal with anything like it. It was because René was leaving her free, and she abhorred her freedom. Her freedom was worse than any conceivable chain. Her freedom was separating her from René. Ten times over, without even saying a word, she could have seized Jacqueline by the shoulders, pinned her to the wall like a butterfly impaled; and Jacqueline wouldn't have budged, doubtless not even smiled. But O was henceforth like one of those wild animals that have been taken captive and either act as the hunter's decoy or chase down the quarry, never leaping until it hears the spoken command. It was she who, pale and trembling, sometimes sank back against a wall, stubbornly impaled by her silence, bound there by her silence, so happy to be silent. She was waiting for more than permission, for that she already had. She was waiting for an order. It came to her not from René, but from Sir Stephen.

With the passing months, ever since the time René had given her to Sir Stephen, O came more and more to see, with increasing terror, the growing importance the Englishman was assuming in the eyes of her lover. It also occurred to her that maybe she was mistaken, that she was perhaps imagining a progression in the fact or the feeling where the only actual progression was in the recognition of this fact or in the acknowledgment of this feeling. Whatever, she had been quick to notice that René chose to spend with her those nights, and only those nights, which followed the evenings when Sir Stephen had summoned her (Sir Stephen keeping her the whole night only when René was away from Paris). She had also noticed that when he remained at one of these evenings, he never touched her unless to help Sir Stephen have her and to maintain her at Sir Stephen's disposition if she struggled. Only very rarely did he stay, and never except at Sir Stephen's express request. At such times, he remained fully clothed, as he had the first time, silent, lighting one cigarette after the other, adding wood to the fire, refilling Sir Stephen's glass—but he himself would not drink. O felt him watch her the way an animal trainer keeps an eye on the animal he has trained, watchful to see that the animal, upon whose performance his honor is at stake, performs perfectly; or even more, the way a prince's bodyguard, or a bandit chieftain's chief lieutenant, watches the prostitute he has gone to fetch out on the street for his master. Evidence that he was indeed yielding to the role of a servant, or of an acolyte, resided in the fact he more closely watched Sir Stephen's face than hers—and whenever he did glance at her, O felt herself stripped of the very joy in which her features were immersed: for this René paid homage, expressed admiration, and even gratitude to Sir Stephen, who was responsible for creating that joy, happy that Sir Stephen had consented to take pleasure in something he had given him.

Surely, everything would have been much simpler if Sir Stephen had been fond of boys, and O had no doubt that René, who wasn't fond of them, would nevertheless have ardently complied with the least and the most trying of Sir Stephen's requests. But Sir Stephen was only fond of women. She realized that through the medium of her mutually shared body they attained something more mysterious, and perhaps more intense, than an amorous communion, to a union the very idea of which made her deeply uncomfortable, but whose reality and strength she could not deny. However, why was this sharing so to speak abstract? At Roissy, O had belonged, at the same instant, in the same place, both to René and to other men. Why in the presence of Sir Stephen did René abstain, not only from taking her, but from issuing orders to her? (All he ever did was transmit Sir Stephen's). She put the question flatly to him, knowing beforehand what he would reply.

"Out of respect," René replied.

"But I belong to you," said O.

"You first of all belong to Sir Stephen."

And it was true, true at least in the sense that when he had abandoned her to his friend, René had abandoned her absolutely, and that Sir Stephen's least desires concerning her took precedence over René's decisions or even over her own. Were René to decide that they'd dine together and go to the theater afterward, and were Sir Stephen then to telephone him an hour before his appointment with O, René would come by for her at the studio as they'd agreed, but it would be to drive her to Sir Stephen's door and leave her there. Once, and only once, O had asked René to beg Sir Stephen to switch it to another day, so much did she want to go to a party to which they had been invited as a couple. "My poor darling," he had said to her, "you mean you still don't understand that you don't belong to me any more, and that the master whom you serve isn't me?" Not only had he refused, but he had communicated O's request to Sir Stephen, and in her presence had asked him to punish her so severely that she'd never again even conceive of shirking her obligations.

"Certainly," Sir Stephen had replied.

The scene took place adjoining the living room, in a little oval room with an inlaid floor, where the only furniture was a mother-of-pearl-encrusted table. René didn't stay long: three minutes, all he needed to betray O and hear Sir Stephen's response, then he shook hands with the latter, smiled at O, and left. Through the window she saw him cross the courtyard, without turning to look back; she heard the car door slam, the motor start, and, in a little mirror set in the wall, she glimpsed her own reflection: her face was white with fear and despair. Then as she walked past Sir Stephen, who had opened the door for her into the living room, she looked at him, mechanically: he was as pale as she. It came in a flash of understanding: the conviction shot through her, and immediately vanished, that he loved her. Although she didn't believe it, and derided herself for having imagined it, it comforted her and she undressed meekly when he gave her the signal. Then—and it was for the first time since he had been making her come to him two or three times a week, gradually wearing her down, sometimes making her wait a full hour, naked, before approaching her, listening to but never making any answer to her pleas, for sometimes she did plead with him, repeating the same injunctions at the same moment, as in a ritual to which he kept so strictly that she knew when her mouth was supposed to caress him and when, kneeling, her head buried in the silk of the couch, she was to offer him now her behind, which he was only able to possess without hurting her, so open to him was she, and it was for the first time, in spite of the fear that gripped her, perhaps in spite of the despair into which René's betrayal had thrown her, she abandoned herself completely. And so for the first time, so submissive were her consenting eyes when they met the burning pale blue eyes of Sir Stephen, he spoke to her in French and in the familiar *tu* form:

"O, I'm going to put a gag in your mouth, for I'd like to whip you till you bleed. Will you allow me to?"

"I am yours," said O.

She was standing in the center of the room, and her upraised arms, which a pair of Roissy bracelets on her wrists held aloft by a chain attached to a ring in the ceiling where once a chandelier had hung, made her breasts thrust forward. Sir Stephen caressed them, then kissed them, then kissed her mouth, once, ten times. (He had never kissed her mouth before.) And when he had applied the gag, which filled her mouth with the taste of wet cloth and which drove her tongue back toward her throat, the gag so arranged that she could scarcely clench it with her teeth, he gently took hold of her hair. Swinging from the chain, she swayed on her bare feet, and almost fell.

"Forgive me, O," he murmured (he had never asked her forgiveness, not even her pardon), then he let go of her, and struck.

René did not return home to O's place until after midnight, after having gone alone to the party at which they both had been expected. He found her in bed, shivering in the white nylon of her long nightgown. Sir Stephen had brought her back and put her to bed himself, and kissed her again. She told René that. She also told him she no longer had any desire not to obey Sir Stephen, realizing as she said this that René would surely conclude that she found it necessary, and agreeable, to be beaten, which was true (but there were other reasons as well). What she was also certain of was that it was equally necessary to René that she be beaten. His dread of beating her was so great that he had never been able to bring himself to do it; no less great was his pleasure at seeing her struggle and at hearing her scream. Sir Stephen had only once used the crop on her in René's presence. René had held her down over the table and had held her still. Her skirt had slid down; he had lifted it up again. Perhaps he had a still greater need to know that while he was not with her, while he was off somewhere on a stroll, or working, O was writhing, groaning, sighing, weeping under the lash, begging for mercy and not having her prayers answered—and knowing that this pain and humiliation were being inflicted on her by the will of the lover who loved her, and for his pleasure. At Roissy, he had her whipped by the valets. In Sir Stephen he had found the stern master he himself did not know how to be. The fact that the man he admired most in the world liked her, and would take the trouble to tame her, only increased, O clearly saw, René's passion. All the mouths that had probed her mouth, all the hands that had grasped her breasts and belly, all the members that had been thrust into her and which had so abundantly demonstrated her prostitution, had simultaneously demonstrated that she was worthy of prostitution and had in some sort sanctified her. But in René's

109

view all that was as nothing compared to the testimonial provided him by Sir Stephen. Each time she emerged from his embrace, René looked for the mark of a god upon her. O knew that if he had betrayed her several hours before, it had been to provoke more, even crueller marks. She also knew that while the reasons for provoking them might disappear, Sir Stephen's reasons for inflicting them would not. A pity. (But, to herself she was thinking precisely the contrary.) Stunned, René stared for a long time at that slender body upon which thick purple welts ran, like so many ropes across shoulders, back, buttocks, belly and breasts, two welts sometimes overlapped and intersected. Here and there a drop or two or blood still oozed through the skin.

"Ah, I love you," he murmured.

His hands trembling, he undressed, turned off the light and lay down close beside O. She moaned in the darkness all the while he possessed her.

The welts on O's body took almost a month to disappear. Even then, in the places where the skin had split, thin, slightly whitish scars remained like ancient vestiges of former scars. But even if she had been able to forget how she had got them, she would have been reminded again by the attitudes of René and Sir Stephen.

Needless to say, René had a key to O's apartment. It had not occurred to him to give a duplicate to Sir Stephen, probably because, until now, Sir Stephen had never evinced the desire to come to O's place. But the fact he had brought her home that evening suddenly made René realize that Sir Stephen might consider this door, which only he and O could open, as an obstacle, as a barrier, as a limitation deliberately imposed by René, and it struck him as ludicrous to

110

give O to Sir Stephen if he also didn't give him free access to her at all times. In short, he had a key made, delivered it to Sir Stephen, and only told O what he had done after Sir Stephen had accepted it. She didn't think of protesting, and as she waited for Sir Stephen to come, she soon discovered an incomprehensible serenity. She waited a good while, wondering whether he would take advantage of one of René's absences, whether he would come alone, whether indeed he would come at all. She didn't dare discuss it with René. One morning when by chance the cleaning woman wasn't there and when she'd got up earlier than usual, and when at ten o'clock, already dressed and ready to go out, she heard a key turn in the lock and rushed to the door, crying: "René!" (for René would sometimes arrive this way, at about this time, and she had been thinking of no one else but him), it was Sir Stephen, who smiled, and said to her: "Let's give him a call."

But René, obliged to stay on at his office because of a business appointment, wouldn't be there for a good hour. O, her heart beating wildly (and she wondering why), watched Sir Stephen hang up the receiver. He had her sit down on the bed, took her head in his hands and opened her mouth slightly to kiss her. The kiss was long and so intense that she could barely breathe, and she might have slipped to the floor had he not been holding her. But he did hold her, and he made her sit erect again. She couldn't understand why she felt so upset, why she was overcome by a wave of anxiety, for, after all, what could she possibly fear at Sir Stephen's hands that she hadn't already experienced? He asked her to remove her clothes, and without a word watched her obey. Wasn't she in fact used to being naked in front of him? Was she not equally accustomed to

111

his silence, to awaiting the decisions of his pleasure? She was obliged to admit to herself that she'd been fooling herself, and that if she was shaken by the time and the place, by the fact that, in this room, she had never been naked except for René, the basic reason for her anxiety was exactly what it always was: this state of being dispossessed of her own self. The only difference was that this dispossession had been brought home to her by the fact that she no longer had any space all to herself in a place where she had been wont to retreat in order to endure it, nor had she any night left to her, nor consequently, any dream or any possibility of clandestine existence: no night to offset the length of the day as Roissy had offset the length of her life with René. That May mornings's bright light made public what had formerly been secret: henceforth, the reality of the night and the reality of the day were going to be one and the same. Henceforth—and, O was thinking, at last. Here in all likelihood was the source of the strange security, mixed with fright, to which she felt she was abandoning herself and which she had somehow sensed without understanding. Henceforth there would be no hiatuses, no dead time, no remission. He for whom one waits, because one awaits him, is already present, already master. Sir Stephen was a more demanding but a surer master than René. And however passionately O might love René, and he her, between the two of them there was an equality (even were it only that of age), which nullified in her the feeling of obedience, the awareness of submission. Whatever he would ask of her she would also want immediately, solely because he had asked it. But one would have thought that he had inculcated in her his own admiration for Sir Stephen, his own respect for him. She obeyed Sir Stephen's orders simply because they were orders, and was grateful to him for giving them to her. Regardless of whether he spoke English or French, addressed her as *tu* or *vous*, she never called him anything but Sir Stephen, as if she were a stranger, or as if she were a servant. She told herself that the word "Lord" would have been more suitable had she dared pronounce it, as it would have been appropriate if, speaking to her, he were to employ the word "slave." She also told herself that all was well, since René was happy to love her as Sir Stephen's slave.

And so, her clothes neatly arranged at the foot of the bed, having put her high-heeled slippers back on, facing Sir Stephen with her eyes lowered, she waited; he was standing at the window. Bright sunshine was pouring through the dotted muslin curtains; already hot, it warmed her loins. O was not interested in striving for effects, but it did immediately occur to her that she ought to have put on more perfume, that she hadn't made up the tips of her breasts, and that it was lucky she had her slippers on, for the polish on her toenails was starting to peel off. Then, all of a sudden, she became aware of what she was actually waiting for, in this silence, in this flood of light, something she hadn't admitted to herself: that Sir Stephen make a signal to her, or order her, to kneel down in front of him, unbutton him and caress him. But no signal, no order was forthcoming. From having thought that of her own accord, she turned red, and as she was blushing she thought herself ridiculous for blushing: what a misplaced modesty in a whore! Just then Sir Stephen invited her to sit down at her dressing table and listen to him. The dressing table was not properly speaking a dressing table but, next to a ledge in the wall upon which were arranged bottles and brushes, a wide, low Restoration table and upon it a mirror where O, in her little armchair, could see herself. As he talked to her, Sir Stephen paced back and forth in the room behind her; from time to time his reflection moved across the mirror, behind O's reflection, but his image seemed faraway, for the silvering of the mirror was discolored and the surface of the glass wavy. O, her hands limp and knees spread, would have liked to seize the reflection, make it stop in order to answer more easily. for, in the most precise English, Sir Stephen was putting question after question to her, the last questions O would ever have dreamed of hearing him ask her, if ever he would have asked any in the first place. Hardly had he begun, however, when he interrupted himself and arranged O so that she was leaning back, almost lying in the chair; her left leg hooked over an arm of the chair, her right bent a little at the knee, in all that flood of light she offered herself, and Sir Stephen, a reflected view of her body as perfectly open as if some invisible lover had withdrawn from her and left her slightly ajar.

Sir Stephen resumed his questioning, with a judges's firmness and the skill of a father-confessor. O did not see him speaking, and she saw herself answer. Had she, since returning from Roissy, belonged to men other than René and himself? No. Had she desired to belong to others whom she might have met? No. Did she caress herself at night at those times when she was alone? No. Did she have any female friends whom she might allow to caress her, or whom she might caress? No (this "no" was more hesitant). But were there any female friends she desired? Well, yes, Jacqueline, except that the word "friend" would be stretching it. "Acquaintance" would be closer to the mark, or even

114

"chum," the way well-brought-up school girls refer to one another in chic boarding schools.

Whereupon Sir Stephen asked her if she had any photographs of Jacqueline, and he helped her to her feet so she could go and fetch them. René, out of breath after running up the four flights, found them in the living room: O, standing beside the large table on which there shone black and white, like puddles of water in the night, all the pictures of Jacqueline. Sir Stephen, half-seated on the edge of the table, was taking them one by one as O handed them to him, and one by one putting them back on the table; his other hand was holding O's womb. As of that moment, Sir Stephen, who had said hello to René without letting go of her—she even felt him bury his fingers deeper into her—ceased to address her, addressing René instead. She clearly saw why: the understanding reached about her, but apart from her, she was simply its occasion or subject, there were no further questions to put to her, no further replies for her to make. What she had to do, and even what she had to be, was being decided without her.

Noon was approaching. The sun, falling directly on the table, was causing the prints to curl at the edge. O wanted to move them into the shade, to flatten them out to prevent them from being ruined; her fingers fumbled, she was close to pleasure's critical point, so persistently did Sir Stephen's fingers probe her. She dropped the pictures, allowed a moan to escape her lips, and found herself lying flat on her back across the table among the scattered photographs where Sir Stephen had rudely pushed her, legs spread and dangling. Her feet didn't reach the floor, one of her slippers fell off, landed noiselessly on the white rug. Her face was bathed in sunlight; she shut her eyes.

115

When, much later, she remembered, she wasn't struck by it, overhearing a conversation between Sir Stephen and René, as if their exchange did not concern her, and at the same time as if experiencing something she'd already lived through. And it was true that she had already experienced a similar scene; for when René had first taken her to Sir Stephen's they had discussed her in the same manner. But that first time she was still a stranger to Sir Stephen, and of the two, René had done most of the talking. Since then, Sir Stephen had molded her to his taste, made her submit to all his fancies, had shaped her to fit him, and it was as a matter of course, unthinkingly, that she had come to comply with his most outrageous demands. There was nothing left for her to cede; he had taken everything already. At least so she thought.

He was speaking, he who usually was silent in her presence, and his words, like those of René, indicated that they had returned to a subject which they often dealt with together, and that subject was she. The question was what to do with her, how to get the most out of her, how to share what each other had learned through his particular use of her. Sir Stephen readily admitted that O was infinitely more exciting when her body was covered with marks, of whatever kind, if only because these marks prevented her from resorting to subterfuges, and immediately proclaimed, to all who saw them, that everything was permitted as far as she was concerned. For knowing it was one thing, visual proof, proof constantly renewed, was quite another. René, Sir Stephen said, had been right in desiring to have her whipped. They decided that, quite apart from the pleasure her screams and tears might afford, she would be flogged as frequently as necessary so that the marks of flog-

116

ging would be visible at all times.

Still lying motionless on her back, her loins still on fire, O listened, and it seemed to her that, by some strange substitution, Sir Stephen was speaking for her, in her place. It was as if he were somehow in her body, as if he had experienced the anxiety, the anguish, the shame, but also the secret pride and the harrowing pleasure she experienced, particularly when she was alone in the midst of strangers, passersby in the street, or when she got into a streetcar or bus, or when she found herself at the studio with the models and technicians, saying to herself that all these people, if they were to meet with some accident, if it were necessary to lay them out on the ground and call a doctor, would keep, even if unconscious, even if naked, their secrets, but not she: her secret wasn't dependent on her silence. Even if she wanted to, she could not indulge the slightest of her whims—and that was just what one of Sir Stephen's questions had meant—without instantly divulging that secret, she could not undertake the most innocent possible activities, playing tennis, or swimming. It was good, it was sweet that these things were forbidden her, materially, as the bars of the convent materially prevent cloistered girls from belonging to one another and from escaping. For this reason, how could she take the chance of not being turned down by Jacqueline without at the same time taking the risk of having to explain to Jacqueline, it not the truth, at least some part of the truth?

The sun had moved and left her face. Her shoulders stuck to the glossy surface of the photographs she was lying on, and against her knee she felt the rough material of Sir Stephen's woolen jacket, for he moved back next to her. René and he each took one of her hands and helped her to

117

her feet. René retrieved her fallen slipper. It was time to get dressed.

It was over lunch at Saint-Cloud, on the banks of the Seine, that Sir Stephen, who had remained alone with her, began to question her again. The restaurant tables, which were covered with white tablecloths, were arranged on a shaded terrace which was surrounded by a private hedge, at the foot of which was a bed of dark red peonies just beginning to reach full bloom.

Even before Sir Stephen could make the sign, she had obediently raised her skirts as she sat down, and it had taken her bare thighs a long time to warm the iron chair. O heard the slapping of the water as it struck the rowboats moored to a jetty of planks at the end of the esplanade. Sir Stephen was sitting opposite her, and O was speaking slowly, determined not to say a word that wasn't true. What Sir Stephen wanted to know was why Jacqueline pleased her. Oh! that was easy: it was because she was too beautiful for O, like the full-sized dolls given as Christmas presents to poor children, which they never dare touch. And at the same time she knew very well that, if she'd never spoken to Jacqueline, never approached her, it was because she'd never really wanted to. Saying that, she raised her eyes, which had been staring at the peonies, and saw that Sir Stephen's eyes were fixed on her lips. Was he listening to her, or had he only been paying attention to the sound of her voice, to the movement of her lips? She suddenly fell silent, and Sir Stephen's gaze rose and intercepted hers. What she read there this time was so clear, and it was so clear to him that she had read it, that it was now his turn to grow pale. If he loved her, how would that change things? If her life had depended on it, she would still not have been capable of making a move, of fleeing, her legs would not have carried her. He would probably never want anything from her but submission to his desires, as long as his desire lasted. But was desire sufficient to explain why, ever since the day René had given her to him, he had asked for her and kept her more and more often, and sometimes simply to have her there, without demanding anything from her? Seated there across from her, he was as silent and still as she; at a neighboring table, some businessmen were holding a discussion while drinking coffee that was so rich and so strong that its aroma wafted all the way over to where they were sitting. Two Americans, smooth-faced, well-groomed and contemptuous, were lighting cigarettes in the middle of their meal; the gravel crunched beneath the steps of the waiters, one of them came over to fill Sir Stephen's glass, which was three-quarters empty, but why pour wine to be drunk by a statue, by a sleepwalker? The waiter went away. Thrilled, O noticed that when his gray, ardent gaze wandered from her eyes; it travelled down to fasten itself on her hands, on her breasts; then it returned to her eyes. At long last she saw the shadow of a smile form on his lips and she dared answer it. But utter a single word? Impossible. She could scarcely breath.

"O . . ." Sir Stephen said.

"Yes," said O in a very faint voice.

"O, what I wanted to talk to you about . . . It's something René and I have discussed and agreed on. But also, I . . ." he broke off.

O never knew whether it was because, stunned, she had closed her eyes, or whether because he too was having trouble breathing. He waited. The waiter changed the dishes, brought O the menu so that she could select a dessert. O handed the menu to Sir Stephen. A soufflé? Yes, a soufflé. That would take twenty minutes. Never mind, let it take twenty minutes, they would have soufflés. The waiter went away.

"I need more than twenty minutes, though," Sir Stephen said. And he went on in a steady voice, and what he said quickly convinced O that at least one thing was certain: that if he loved her, nothing was going to be changed, unless one could consider a change this curious respect, this ardor with which he was telling her: "I'd be very happy if you'd like . . . " instead of simply inviting her to accede to his requests. Nevertheless, these were still orders, which there wasn't the slightest question of O disobeying. She brought this to Sir Stephen's attention. He admitted it was true. "But answer all the same," he said.

"I will do whatever you like," replied O, and the echo of what she'd just said resounded in her memory: "I will do what you like," she had told René. She murmured: "René . . . "

Sir Stephen heard it.

"He knows what I would like from you. Listen to me."

He was speaking English now, in a low, muffled voice that was inaudible to the adjoining tables. Whenever waiters approached, he fell silent, until they moved away, at which point he picked up precisely where he had left off. What he was saying seemed incredibly out of keeping in the context of this public, peaceful place, and yet the most incredible of all was without a doubt that he could say it, and O hear it, in such a natural manner.

He began by reminding her that when she'd come to him that first evening he had given her an order which she had not obeyed, and he further reminded her that, although he

120

might have slapped her then, he had never repeated the same order since. Would she grant him from now on what she had refused him then? O understood that it wasn't just that she had to acquiesce, but that he wanted to hear her say with her own lips and in her own words that, yes, she would caress herself whenever he asked her to. She said it, and once again saw the yellow and gray drawing room, René's departure, her revolt of that first evening, the fire glowing between her open knees when she was lying naked on the rug. This evening, in that same drawing room . . . . But no, Sir Stephen didn't specify, and returned to what he had been saying.

He also pointed out to her that she had never, in his presence, been possessed by René (nor by anyone else), as she had been in René's presence by him (and, at Roissy, by a good many other men.) From this she ought not to conclude that René would be the only one to inflict on her the humiliation of giving her to a man who didn't love her—and perhaps of deriving pleasure from it—in the presence of someone who loved her. (He went on at great length and was so adamant, he assured her that she would soon open her belly and behind and her mouth to any of his friends who might desire her when once they had met her; and O was led to wonder whether this vehemence was not addressed as much to him as to her, and only the end of the sentence stuck in her mind: "in the presence of someone who loved her." What more could she ask for by way of confession?) Furthermore, he himself would take her back to Roissy in the course of the summer. Had she never wondered at the isolation in which first René, then he, Sir Stephen, kept her? She saw no one else, only they, either together or separately. When Sir Stephen entertained in his

121

house on the rue de Poitiers, he never invited O. Never had she lunched or dined at his place. Nor had René ever introduced her to any of his friends except Sir Stephen. He would in all likelihood continue to keep her away from others, for Sir Stephen had the privilege of disposing her. However, she shouldn't for a moment think that, while being his, she'd be less under private charter; on the contrary. (But what hurt O most was that Sir Stephen was going to be with her as René had been, exactly, identically.) The ring of iron and gold she wore on her left hand—and did she remember that they had chosen so tight-fitting a ring that she had had to force it onto her finger? She had not be able to remove it—was the sign she was a slave, and a common one to boot. It had been by mere chance that since this past autumn she had not met any Roissy affiliates who could have taken notice of her ring-symbolized servitude, of her irons, or shown their recognition.

The word irons, used in the plural, in which she had detected an ambiguity when Sir Stephen had said irons became her so, was not by any means an ambiguity but a password. He had not had to use the other formula, that is, whose irons are you wearing? But if the question were put to her today, what would she answer? O hesitated.

"To René and to you," she said.

"No," said Sir Stephen. "To me. René wants you to be answerable to me first and foremost." O knew it; why was she pretending she didn't? In a little while, at any rate before returning to Roissy, she would accept a definitive mark which would not absolve her from common slavery, but would designate her, among other things, as a particular individual's slave, Sir Stephen's, and compared to which the traces left on her body by a whip or a riding crop, no matter how often repeated, would be unobtrusive and superfluous. (But what kind of mark, what was it to consist of, in what way would it be definitive? Terrified, fascinated, O was dying to know, and to know right now. But apparently Sir Stephen was not yet ready to explain. And it was true that she would have to consent, in the true sense of the word, for nothing would be forcibly inflicted on her without her having agreed to it first. She could refuse, for nothing obliged her to remain a slave, nothing except her love and slavery itself. What prevented her from leaving, from getting completely out of this?) However, before this mark was imposed on her, even before Sir Stephen were to make it a habit—as it had been decided between him and René—that he would so schedule her whippings that traces of them would always be visible on her body, she would be granted a reprieve—time enough for her to induce Jacqueline to submit to him. At this point O, who was stunned, looked up and stared at Sir Stephen. Why? Why Jacqueline? And if Sir Stephen was interested in Jacqueline, what did this have to do with O?

"There are two reasons," said Sir Stephen. "The first and less important is that I want to see you embrace and caress a woman."

"But how in heaven's name," O exclaimed, "Even if we assume she were to take me, how would I get her to consent to your being present?"

"There's nothing to it," Sir Stephen said. "Any way you like. By betrayal if necessary, and I am counting on you to get considerably more than that out of her. The second reason I want her to be yours is that you are to induce her—lure her, if you like—into going to Roissy."

O set down the coffee cup she was holding in her hand,

which was trembling so violently that she ended up spilling the cup's dregs and a little sugar, onto the tablecloth. As though she were a soothsayer, she saw in the spreading brown stain appalling images: the terrified eyes of Jacqueline confronted by the valet Pierre, her flanks, doubtless as golden as her breasts, haunches O had never seen but which she now imagined in an offered position, framed by her great red velvet robe, which was tucked up, tears streaming down her cheeks, her painted mouth wide open and screaming, and her hair straight as straw falling down over her brow—no, it was impossible, not her, not Jacqueline.

"It can't be done," she said.

"Yes it can," Sir Stephen replied. "And how do you suppose girls are recruited for Roissy? Once you've brought her there, nothing more will be asked of you—and if she wants to leave, she'll leave. Now, come along."

He had gotten suddenly to his feet, leaving a wad of bank notes on the table to pay for the bill. O followed him to the car, stepped in, and sat down. They had gone only a little way into the Bois de Boulogue when he veered off into a side road, parked in a little lane, and took her in his arms.

3

Anne-Marie and the Rings

O had believed, or preferred to believe in order to give herself an excuse, that Jacqueline would be uncommonly shy. She was disabused the moment she chose to open her eyes.

Jacqueline's modest airs—closing the door of the little room with the mirror where she put on and took off her dresses—were clearly meant to intrigue O, to excite her desire to break down a door which, wide open, she could not make up her mind to enter. That O's decision was finally not her own but dictated to her by an outside authority, and did not result from this elementary strategy, was furthest from Jacqueline's mind. This amused O at first. While helping Jacqueline arrange her hair, for example, when, having taken off the clothes she had been posing in, she put on her turtle-neck sweater and the turquoise necklace, whose stones matched the color of her eyes, O took extraordinary pleasure in thinking that Sir Stephen would, that same evening, obtain complete information regarding all of Jacqueline's reactions: whether Jacqueline had let her fondle those two small, well-separated breasts through the folds of the black sweater; whether she had lowered those eyelids,

127

whose lashes were even lighter than her golden skin; whether she had moaned with pleasure. When O kissed her, Jacqueline became heavy, very still, and as though expectant in her arms, parted her lips, tossed her hair to one side. O always had to be careful to thrust her up against a doorway or against the edge of a table and to anchor her shoulders. Otherwise Jacqueline would have slipped to the floor, her eyes shut, without a sound. The minute O released her, she turned back into a creature of frost and snow, laughing and distant, saying: "You've got lipstick on me," and would wipe her mouth. This was the foreign, the distant person O loved to betray by taking such exact note—so as to forget nothing and be able to relate it all—of the slow flush that would rise to the girl's cheeks, of the odor of sweat and sage about her. One couldn't very well say that Jacqueline was defensive or mistrustful. When she yielded to kisses—and, until now, she had not granted O anything beyond kisses, letting herself be kissed but not kissing in return—she yielded all of a sudden and, it seemed, completely, all at once becoming someone else for the space of ten seconds, of five minutes. The rest of the time she was simultaneously provocative and coquettish, incredibly skillful at parrying and evasions, never failing to maintain a situation which, forever fluid, eliminated any possibility for a gesture or a word or even a glance which might have revealed the victor's conquest or allowed O to suppose that Jacqueline's besieged mouth wanted only to surrender. The only indication by which one could be guided, and perhaps suspect the troubled waters that lay beneath the still surface of her gaze, was that occasional shadow of an involuntary smile on her triangular face, similar to a cat's smile, and, like a cat's, indecisive and fleeting, puzzling and disturbing. Yet it did not take O long to realize that two things could produce it, and that Jacqueline was aware of neither. First, the gifts she presented her. Second, clear evidence of the desire she aroused in someone—provided, though, that this someone who desired her might be useful to her, or flattered her vanity. In what way, then, was O of use to her? Or could it be that Jacqueline simply found pleasure in being desired by O both because the admiration O displayed for her was consoling or reassuring and because a woman's desire can neither be dangerous nor have consequences? Still, O was convinced that if, instead of bringing Jacqueline a mother-of-pearl clip or the latest Hermes scarf with "I Love You" printed all over it in every language under the sun, she had offered Jacqueline the ten or twenty thousand francs she constantly seemed to need, Jacqueline would have stopped never having time to join O for lunch, or for tea at O's place, or stopped evading her caresses. But O never had proof of it. Barely had she spoken about what was going on to Sir Stephen, and heard his reproaches for allowing things to progress too slowly, than René stepped in. The five or six times René had come by for O at the studio when Jacqueline had been there too, they'd all gone out together, either to Weber's or to one of the English bars in the vicinity of the Madeleine; René would observe Jacqueline with precisely that same mixture of interest, self-confidence, and insolence with which he would gaze at the girls who were at his complete disposal at Roissy. Insolence slid harmlessly and completely unnoticed off Jacqueline's armor. By a curious contradiction, O was upset by it, viewing as insulting to Jacqueline an attitude she found perfectly correct and natural when it came to her. Was she considering taking up Jacqueline's defense, or did she simply want Jacqueline all to herself? She really couldn't have told which, all the more so because she didn't possess Jacqueline—at least not yet. But if she finally did succeed, it must be said that it was owing to René. On three occasions, leaving the bar where he had had Jacqueline drink a good deal more whisky than she ought to have—her cheeks became flushed, her eyes hard—he had dropped her off at her place before continuing on with O to Sir Stephen's.

Jacqueline lived in one of those somber *pensions de famille* into which the White Russians had piled in the early days of the emigration and from which they had never subsequently moved. The vestibule was painted in imitation oak, the stairway's balustrades were full of dust, and great pale patches showed where the green stair carpeting had been worn down. Every time René—who had never got past the front door—wanted to come in, Jacqueline always shouted "No thanks," jumped out of the car, and slammed the door of the house behind her, as if some tongue of fire had suddenly shot forth and burned her. And it was true: she was being pursued by fire, O would say to herself. She was to be admired for having guessed it, even though there was no way she could really have known. Jacqueline at least seemed to know that she had to be on her guard with René, whose detachment appeared not to affect her at all (or did it? and insofar as being unaffected, two could play at that game, and he was a worthy opponent for her). The only time Jacqueline had let her enter the house and follow her up to her room, O had understood why she so adamantly refused to allow René into the place. What would have happened to her prestige, to the black-and-white legend on the slick pages of expensive fashion magazines, if someone other than a woman like O had ever seen from what sordid den the glorious beast issued forth every morning? The bed was never made, the bedclothes were hardly even pulled up, the sheet one glimpsed was dirty and greasy, for Jacqueline never went to bed without massaging her face with cold cream and then went to sleep too quickly to think of wiping it off. Some time back a curtain must have separated the toilet from the room; now all that remained were two rings on a bent curtain rod from which hung a couple of shreds of cloth. The color was faded out of everything; there was none left in the rug or in the wallpaper in which red and gray flowers climbed like vegetation gone mad and become petrified on a fake white trellis. You would have had to make a clean sweep, rip everything down, scrape the walls bare, throw out the rug, sand the floor. But in any case immediately get rid of those lines of filth which like so many encrusted layers striped the enamel of the washbowl; clean and put some order into the jars of make-up and make-up remover, the pots, the bottles; wipe off the powder box, sweep up the loose hair, throw away the dirty cotton and open the windows. But straight as a willow wand, as cool and clean as one and smelling of wild flowers, impeccable, spotless, Jacqueline didn't give a damn about her hovel. On the other hand, what she did give a damn about, what weighed on her, was her family. It was because of the "hovel," about which O had spoken to René in all frankness, that he made the suggestion to O which was to change their lives but which, when it had been put to her as a proposal, Jacqueline agreed to because of her family. The suggestion was that Jacqueline move in with O. "Family" was hardly the word for it: this was a tribe, or rather a horde. Grandmother, aunt, mother, and even a maid, four women ranging in age between fifty and seventy, all screaming at the same time, all too heavily made up, all smothered under their black silks and ornaments, sobbing at four in the morning in the cigarette smoke and faint red glow of icons, four women in the click of glasses of tea and the hissing of a language Jacqueline would have given half her life to forget—she was going crazy from having to obey them, listen to them, and from simply having to see them. Whenever she saw the way her mother would pop a lump of sugar into her mouth before taking a swallow of tea, she would set down her own glass, retreat to her dry and dusty little pigsty, leaving the three of them behind—grandmother, mother, and mother's sister—all three dark, with hair dyed black and eyebrows that met at the bridge of the nose, with great reproachful doe-eyes—there in her mother's room, which served as their salon and in which the maid ended up resembling them. She retreated, she fled, banging the doors behind her, and in her wake there'd come cries of "Choura, Choura, little dove, little dove," just as in Tolstoy's novels, for her name wasn't Jacqueline. Jacqueline was a professional name, a name for her job and for forgetting her real name and, along with her real name, this sordid and heartbreaking gyneceum, for getting a place in the sun, at least in the French world, in a more or less solid world where men exist who marry you and who don't disappear in mysterious expeditions the way her father had—her father whom she had never known, a Baltic sailor who had succumbed somewhere in the Arctic wastes. She looked exactly like him, she told herself with a mixture of rage and delight, she had his hair and his high cheekbones; his complexion and his slanting eyes. The one thing she felt grateful to her mother for was for having given her that blond demon for a father whom the snows had reclaimed as earth reclaims other men. But what she did not forgive her mother for was for having forgotten him to the point of one fine day giving birth—the result of a short-lived affair—to a dark-skinned little girl, her half-sister by an unknown father, who had been named Nathalie. Nathalie was to be seen only during vacation time. Her father never. But he footed the bill for Nathalie's schooling in a lycée not far from Paris, and gave Nathalie's mother an allowance, not much, but enough to assure a mediocre existence, in the idleness which was their paradise, to the three women and to the maid—and even to Jacqueline, up until now. What Jacqueline earned from her profession, from her job as a model, that is whatever remained after what she spent in cosmetics or lingerie or in shoes bought at a chic shop or in outfits created by some top fashion designer—she got them at a discount, since she was in the business; but even so, the prices were still very steep—vanished into the family's purse, or simply vanished, God knows where.

Jacqueline could certainly have found a lover, and she had her fair share of opportunities. She had in fact had one or two lovers, less because they pleased her—they hadn't in fact displeased her—than to prove to herself that she was capable of inspiring desire and love. The only one of the two—the second—who was rich, had made her a present of a very handsome, slightly pink pearl ring which she wore on her left hand, but she had refused to live with him, and since he had refused to marry her she had left him, with no great regrets, relieved at not being pregnant (she had thought she was, had lived in dread for several days). No, living with a lover was to lose face, to lose one's chances for a future, to do what her mother had done with the father of Nathalie, and that was impossible. But with O, well, that was another story. A polite fiction would give the impression that Jacqueline was simply moving in with a girlfriend, and sharing the place and costs with her. O would serve two purposes at once, would play two roles: that of the lover who supports, or helps the girl he loves, and the theoretically contrary role of a moral guarantee. René's presence wasn't official enough to compromise the fiction. But in the background of Jacqueline's decision—who can say whether or not that same presence hadn't been the real motive for her acceptance? At any rate, it was up to O, and to O alone, to propose the idea to Jacqueline's mother. Never before had O felt so intensely what it feels like to be a traitor, a spy, the envoy of a criminal organization, as when she found herself face to face with that woman who thanked O for her kindness to her daughter. At the same time, in the depths of her heart, O was saying no to her mission and to the reason she was there. Yes, Jacqueline would come to stay with her, but O would never, never be able to acquiesce to Sir Stephen to the point of putting her into his clutches. And yet! .... For no sooner had Jacqueline moved into the apartment— where, and it was at René's request, she was given the room which he sometimes made a semblance of occupying (a bare semblance, in the light of the fact he always slept in O's big bed)—than O most unexpectedly found herself prey to an overwhelming desire to possess Jacqueline at any price, even if that meant surrendering her to Sir Stephen. After all, she said to herself, Jacqueline's beauty was more than sufficient to protect her; why should I interfere? And if she is to be reduced to what I am reduced to, is that really so terrible? All this while she fought not to admit, and yet trembled as she imagined, the immense joy she would feel in seeing

134

Jacqueline at her side, like her, naked and defenseless, like her.

In the course of the same week Jacqueline moved in, full permission having been given by her mother, René made a point of celebrating the new situation, inviting both of them out to dinner and taking them to see films which, oddly, he selected from what was showing of recent thrillers, stories of drug trafficking or white slavery. He would sit between them, gently hold hands with them both, and not say a word. But during any violent scene O saw him glancing out of the corner of his eye at Jacqueline, watching for some sign of emotion on her face. But the only thing you could see on Jacqueline's face was a trace of disgust, which lowered the corners of her mouth.

Afterward René would drive them home, and in the car, the convertible top down and the windows down as well, the night wind and the speed blew Jacqueline's thick blond hair down over her firm cheeks and over her narrow forehead and even into her eyes. She tossed her head, flipping back her hair, brushing it back with her hand the way boys do. Once she had accepted the fact that she was living at O's, and that O was René's mistress, Jacqueline, advancing from these premises, seemed to proceed logically to the conclusion that René's familiarities were perfectly natural. Without flinching, she accepted the idea that René might enter her room under the pretense that he had left some document there, which, O knew, wasn't true, for she herself had emptied all the drawers of the tall Dutch secretary, with its flowery inlay and leather-surfaced hinged top always open, a desk so out of keeping with René. Why did he have it? Where had he got it? Its heavy elegance, its light contrasting woods were the only touch of luxury in the rather dark room which faced north onto the court, and whose walls were steel gray, and whose cold waxed wooden floor contrasted so sharply with the cheerful rooms looking out onto the quay. All well and good. Jacqueline wouldn't like it there. She would all the more readily agree to share the two front rooms with O, to sleep with O, as she had agreed the very first day to share the bathroom and the kitchen, the cosmetics, the perfumes, and the meals. In all this O was mistaken. Jacqueline was passionately attached to whatever belonged to her—to her rose-colored pearl ring, for example—but absolutely indifferent to what wasn't hers. Lodged in a palace, she would only have become interested in her surroundings if she had been told that the palace belonged to her and if proof of ownership had been presented to her in the form of a notarized deed. Whether the gray room was pleasant or not, it was all the same to her, and it was not to escape from it that she came to sleep in O's bed. Nor was it to demonstrate to O a gratitude she did not feel, but which, nevertheless, O ascribed to her, being at the same time delighted to abuse it, and she did think that she was abusing it. Jacqueline liked pleasure, and found it both agreeable and practical to receive it from a woman, in whose hands she ran no risks.

Five days after having unpacked her suitcases and with O's help arranged what had been in them, and when René had brought them home for the third time, about ten o'clock, and had then left, as he had the two times before, she appeared in O's doorway, naked and still damp from her bath, and said: "You're sure he's not coming back?" and without even waiting for her answer, she slipped into the big bed. She let herself be embraced and caressed, her eyes shut. She did not respond with a single caress; at first she

136

moaned slightly, then still louder, and finally gave a cry, She fell asleep, the light of the pink lamp falling on her face, her body sprawled across the bed, knees apart, torso a bit to one side, hands open. The sweat glistened in the cleft between her breasts. O drew the covers over her and turned out the light. Two hours later, when she took Jacqueline again, in the darkness, Jacqueline acquiesced, but murmured: "Don't tire me out too much, I have to get up early tomorrow."

This was the period when Jacqueline, in addition to her intermittent jobs as a model, took up the equally unpredictable but more absorbing work of playing bit parts in movies. It was difficult to tell whether or not she was proud of being an actress, whether or not she saw these small roles as the first step of a career in which she might have wanted to make a name for herself. More with rage than with enthusiasm, she would drag herself out of bed in the morning, take a shower and make up quickly, swallowing nothing but the big cup of black coffee O would barely have time to get ready for her. She would give her fingertips to O to kiss, put on a mechanical smile, and glower: O was sweet and warm in her white bathrobe, her hair brushed, her face washed, with the air of someone about to go back to bed for a few more hours sleep. However, it wasn't true. O hadn't yet found the courage to explain why to Jacqueline. The truth was that every day Jacqueline left the apartment on her way to the movie studios in Bologne where her film was being shot, at the hour children set off for school and white-collar workers left for their offices, O, who in the past had indeed spent most of the morning at home, would get dressed too: "I'm sending my car," Sir Stephen had said. It will take Jacqueline to Bologne and then come back and pick

137

you up." O found herself arriving at Sir Stephen's every morning at an hour when the sun was still only striking the eastern façades; the other walls were still cold, but the shadows in the gardens would be shortening.

At the rue de Poitiers, morning tidying-up was still underway. Norah, the maid, would escort O to the little room where, the first evening, Sir Stephen had let her sleep and cry by herself, would wait until O had taken off her gloves and set them with her bag and clothes on the bed, then take them and, while O looked on, put them in a closet to which she alone had the key; then, having given O her high-heeled slippers which clicked when she walked, would precede her, opening one door after another for her, until they came to the door of Sir Stephen's study, where she would step aside to allow O to pass. O never got used to these preparations, and taking off all her clothes in front of this patient old woman who seldom looked at her, and never said anything to her, was as much of an ordeal as being naked in front of the valets at Roissy. In felt slippers, the elderly woman drifted here and there in silence like a nun. As she followed her, O could not take her eyes off the two points of her madras kerchief and, every time she opened a door, her thin brown hand, seemingly as hard as the wood, on the porcelain doorknob. At the same time, together with the awe she felt in Norah's presence, there was another, entirely opposite, but not, O thought, contradictory feeling: she derived a certain pride from the fact that this servant of Sir Stephen (what, exactly, was her relation to Sir Stephen? his view of her? why had he entrusted her with this role of dresser, which she seemed so poorly suited for?) was witness that she too—like others, perhaps, whom she likewise guided about the apartment and attended to, who knows?—was worthy of being utilized by Sir Stephen. For perhaps Sir Stephen was in love with her, yes, surely he did love her, and O sensed that the time was not far off when he was not simply going to let her think so, but to tell her so—but insofar as his love and desire for her were increasing, so his demands on her were becoming more extensive, more exacting, more minute. Thus retained at his side for whole mornings, during which he sometimes scarcely touched her, wishing only to be caressed by her, she did as he bid, to satisfy him with what can only be called gratitude, which was all the greater when his wishes took on the form of an order. Each wish she surrendered to was her guarantee that another surrender would be required of her, each of his wishes she complied with was for her like some duty duly performed; how strange, that she should have found this completely fulfilling; yet for her it was.

Sir Stephen's office, located on the floor below the yellow and gray drawing room he used in the evening, was less spacious and had a lower ceiling. Here there was neither settee nor couch, only two Regency armchairs upholstered in a floral pattern. Sometimes O sat down in one of them, but Sir Stephen generally preferred to have her nearer to him, at arm's length, and while his attentions was absorbed in other matters, to have her sit on his desk, to his left. The desk was at right angles to the wall, O could lean her back against shelves containing dictionaries and leather-bound telephone books. The telephone was next to her left thigh, and she jumped every time it rang. It was she who would pick up the receiver and answer, asking: "Who is it, please?" and repeating the caller's name aloud; she would then either put Sir Stephen on the line or, depending on what he signaled to her, make up some excuse why he could not take the call.

Whenever a visitor arrived, Norah announced him; then Sir Stephen had the visitor wait long enough for Norah to be able to take O back to the room where she had undressed and where, after the visitor had left, Norah came to fetch her again when Sir Stephen rang for her.

Since Norah came in and out of the study several times every morning, to bring Sir Stephen coffee or the mail or to empty ashtrays, and since she alone had the right to enter, having been instructed never to knock, and, finally, since when she had something to say she always waited in silence for Sir Stephen to inquire what it was she wanted, it so happened on one occasion that O was bent over the desk, her head and elbows resting on the leather top, her rump raised in the air, waiting to be penetrated by Sir Stephen, at the very moment Norah entered. O raised her head. If Norah had not looked at her—and she never did—that would have been the only movement O would have made. But this time it was evident that Norah wanted to catch O's glance. The woman's dark eyes fastened on her own, and O had no way of knowing whether she was indifferent; those eyes, in that deep-lined and expressionless face, so startled O that she made an involuntary movement to escape from Sir Stephen. He understood; he pressed one hand down hard upon her back to prevent her from slipping away, and pried her open with the other. She who always made every effort to please was now, despite herself, tense and contracted, and Sir Stephen had to force his way into her. Even after he had done so, she felt the ring of her buttocks squeeze tight around him, and he had considerable trouble thrusting himself all the way in. He did not withdraw until he was able to move backward and forward without difficulty. Then, as he was about to take her again, he told Norah to wait, that she

140

could dress O when he was finished with her. However, before sending her off, he kissed O tenderly on the lips. It was thanks to that kiss that, several days later, she found the courage to tell him that Norah frightened her.

"I should hope so," he said. "And when you wear, as you shortly shall—if you consent—my mark and my irons, you'll have much more reason to fear her."

"Why?" O asked. "What mark? What irons? I already wear this ring—"

"All that is Anne-Marie's business. I've promised to show you to her. We're going to see her after lunch. She is one of my friends, and I suppose you've noticed that, until now, I have never introduced you to any of them. When Anne-Marie is finished with you, I'll give you some very sound reasons for being afraid of Norah."

O didn't dare pursue the matter any further. She was intrigued even more by this Anne-Marie than by Norah. It was of her Sir Stephen had spoken during their lunch at Saint-Cloud. And it was true that O knew none of Sir Stephen's friends, none of his acquaintances. Locked in her secret, she was living in Paris as though in a brothel; the only people who had a right to her secret, René and Sir Stephen, at the same time had the right to her body. It occurred to her that the words "open oneself to someone," which meant to confide oneself, had, in their application to her, but one meaning: quite literal, physical, but nevertheless absolute and essential, for the fact was that she opened herself in every part of her body which could possibly open. It also seemed that therein lay her *raison d'être*, and that, like René, Sir Stephen so construed her *raison d'être*, since when he spoke of his friends, as he had at Saint-Cloud, it was to tell her that those whom he was going to introduce her to

141

would as a matter of course be entitled to dispose of her body if they so desired. But trying to visualize Anne-Marie, and imagine what Sir Stephen expected of Anne-Marie, O had nothing, as far as she was concerned, to go on, not even her Roissy experience. Sir Stephen had also told her that he wanted to see her caress a woman—was this it? (But he had specified that it was to be Jacqueline . . . .) No, that wasn't it. He had just said "to show you." But when O left Anne-Marie, she still did not know.

Anne-Marie lived near the Observatoire in Paris in an apartment flanked by a kind of large studio, on the top floor of a new building overlooking the tree tops. She was a small, thin woman, Sir Stephen's age, and her black hair was streaked with gray. Her eyes were blue, but of such a deep blue they could easily be mistaken for black. She offered Sir Stephen and O some very strong coffee in tiny cups: boiling hot, bitter coffee. It comforted O. When she had finished drinking it and had risen from her chair to lay her empty cup down on the table, Anne-Marie caught her by the wrist and, turning to Sir Stephen, asked: "May I?"

"By all means," Sir Stephen said.

Whereupon Anne-Marie, who until then, even on greeting her visitors, even when Sir Stephen had introduced O to her, had not uttered a word to her nor even smiled in her direction, now spoke to her softly and smiled so warmly that one might have thought she was giving O a present:

"Come, my child, let me see your belly and your buttocks. But better yet, take off your clothes first."

While O was obeying, Anne-Marie lit a cigarette. Sir Stephen's eyes had not once left O. They left her standing there for some time, perhaps five minutes. There was no

142

mirror in the room, but O caught a vague reflection of herself in the bright surface of a black lacquered screen.

"Take off your stockings, too." Anne-Marie suddenly said. "You see," she went on, "look at your thighs. You're going to spoil them by wearing those garters," and, with her fingertip she drew O's attention to the very faint crease which, a little above her knee, designated the place where O rolled her stockings around a wide elastic garter.

"Who told you to do that?"

Before O could answer: "The young fellow who gave her to me, you know," said Sir Stephen, "René. But," he added, "he'll certainly agree with you. Never fear."

"Very well," said Anne-Marie; and then, to O: "I am going to give you some long dark stockings, and a corset to hold them up. But it will be a whalebone corset, snug at your waist."

Anne-Marie had rung, and a blond, silent girl had come back with some fine sheer black stockings and a short corset of black nylon taffeta, held rigid by wide, close-set whalebone stays curving inward below the buttocks and around in front too. O, still standing, shifting awkwardly from one foot to the other, slipped on the stockings which came all the way up to the top of her thighs. The blond girl helped her into the corset, which buckled to one side and near the rear. Also at the rear, as with the Roissy bodices, were laces to adjust the fit as loosely or as tightly as desired. O hooked her stockings in front and at the side by four garter-belt snaps, then the girl laced her up as tightly as possible. O felt her waist and belly forced inward by the pressure of the stays which, in front, reached almost down to her pubis, leaving it free however, as it did her entire buttocks.

"She'll be much better," said Anne-Marie, addressing Sir

143

Stephen, "when her waist is greatly reduced. What's more, if you're in too much of a hurry to get her undressed, you'll find the corset won't be an inconvenience. Will you step this way, O."

The girl left the room, O went toward Anne-Marie who was sitting in a low chair covered in bright red velvet. Anne-Marie's hand strayed softly over her buttocks, then, making her bend down over a hassock—also covered with the same red velvet—raised her buttocks and spread her legs and, ordering her not to move, seized both her nether lips. This, O said to herself, is how they open the gills of fish at the market, and pull open the mouths of horses to show you the teeth. She also remembered that the valet Pierre, the first evening at Roissy, after he'd chained her, had done the same thing. But after all she was no longer her own person, and what belonged to her least of all was, most assuredly, the half of her body which could, as it were, be put to use independently of the rest of her. Why then, each time she realized this, was she not so much surprised at the discovery but as if persuaded of the fact; why, each time, was she the subject to the same deep distress which paralyzed her and put her not so much into the hands of him who took her as into those of him who gave her to the use of some stranger, which, at Roissy, delivered her to René when the others were possessing her, and here—to whom? To René, or Sir Stephen? Oh, she no longer knew. But that was because she didn't want to know anymore, for it was very surely to Sir Stephen she belonged and had belonged ever since—ever since when?

Anne-Marie had her stand up and get dressed.

"You can bring her to me whenever you like," she told Sir Stephen, "I'll be at Samois."

Samois? O had been expecting to hear Roissy; but it wasn't Roissy; so what was it then?

"In two days. That will be fine." (What would be fine?)

"In ten days, if that suits you," Sir Stephen replied, "at the beginning of July."

Sir Stephen having remained behind at Anne-Marie's, O, as she was being driven home, remembered the statue she'd seen as a child in the Luxembourg Gardens; a woman whose waist had been similarly compressed, whose waist seemed so slim between her heavy breasts and plump behind—the stone woman had been bending forward, gazing at her reflection in a spring, also of marble and meticulously sculptured at her feet—that she'd been afraid the marble would snap in two. Well, if that was what Sir Stephen wanted . . . . As for Jacqueline, it would be very easy to tell her that all this was simply one of René's whims. A nagging thought she'd tried to flee every time it came back to her, and which, nevertheless, she was always surprised to find less painful than it perhaps ought to have been: why, since Jacqueline had come to live with her, had René taken such care not only to leave her alone with Jacqueline, which she could understand, but to avoid being alone with her, O? July was fast approaching, and René was to leave in July, he wouldn't come to see her at this place where Sir Stephen was sending her to be with this Anne-Marie person; was she therefore going to have to resign herself to not seeing him except on those evenings when he was inclined to invite Jacqueline and her out, or—and she didn't know which of the two was the more upsetting (since at this point between the two of them there was something basically false about their relationship, due to the fact that the relationship was so limited)—sometimes during the morning when she was

145

with Sir Stephen, and when Norah announced René's arrival and then ushered him in? Sir Stephen received regular visits from René, who always kissed O, caressed the tips of her breasts, discussed with Sir Stephen plans for the next day—plans which did not involve her—and then left. Had he so thoroughly given her to Sir Stephen that he had reached the stage of not loving her anymore? What was going to happen if he didn't love her anymore? O was overwhelmed by such a feeling of panic that, mechanically, she got out without thinking on the quay in front of her house and, instead of keeping the car, sent it on its way and had to dash off to find a taxi. There aren't many taxis on the quay de Bethune. She ran all the way to the Boulevard Saint-Germain and then had to wait for quite some time. She was in a sweat, all out of breath, for her corset was making it hard for her to breath. And then at last a taxi did slow down at the corner of the rue du Cardinal-Lemoine. She flagged down the driver, gave him the address of the office where René worked, got in, without knowing whether René would be there, whether he'd see her, if in fact he was there, she'd never gone to his office before. She was surprised neither by the imposing building on a street leading off the Champs-Elysees nor by the American-style offices; but the attitude of René, who did have her come in right away, did disconcert her. Not that he was aggressive, or full of reproaches. She would have preferred reproaches, for, after all, he had not given her permission to interrupt him that way, and it was, perhaps a considerable disturbance for him. He sent his secretary out, told her he did not want to be interrupted and to hold all calls. Then he asked O what the matter was.

"I was afraid, that you didn't love me anymore," said O.

He laughed. "All of a sudden, just out of a clear blue sky ?"

"Yes, in the car coming back . . . back from—"

"From where?"

O said nothing. René laughed again.

"But," he said. "I know where you were, silly girl. You were coming back," he laughed, "from Anne-Marie's apartment. And you're going to Samois in ten days. Sir Stephen just called me."

René was sitting in the only comfortable chair in his office, which was facing the table, and O was buried in his arms. "I don't care what they do with me," she murmured. "But tell me you still love me."

"My darling creature," he said, "I do love you. But I want you to obey me and you don't, at least not very well. You've told Jacqueline that you belong to Sir Stephen, you've talked to her about Roissy?"

O assured him that she had not. Jacqueline accepted her caresses, but the day she knew that O . . . .

René stopped her from finishing her sentence, lifted her up, leaned her against the chair he'd just got up from, then raised her skirt.

"Ah, ha, there's the corset," he mused. "It's true, you'll be much more attractive when your waist is slimmer."

Then he took her, and it struck O that it had been such a long time since he'd done it that, she realized, she had even begun to doubt whether he still wanted her, and in this she found proof of his love.

"You know," he said to her afterward, "you're foolish not to talk to Jacqueline. We need her at Roissy, though the best way to get her there would be through you. Anyway, when you come back from Anne-Marie's your true condition will speak for itself, you'll no longer be able to hide it.

O asked why.

147

"You'll see," said René. "You still have five days, and only five, for five days before he sends you to Anne-Marie, Sir Stephen intends to begin whipping you again every day. You'll surely show traces of it, and how will you explain them to Jacqueline?"

O did not reply. What René did not know was that Jacqueline was interested in her only because of O's passion for her, and otherwise never even glanced at her. If she were to be covered with welts from the flogging, she'd have only to be careful not to bathe while Jacqueline was there, and to wear a nightgown. She hadn't noticed that O didn't wear panties; she wouldn't notice anything: O simply didn't interest her.

"Listen," René said, "there is at any rate one thing I want you to tell her and tell her right away: that I'm in love with her."

"Is that true?" O asked.

"I want to have her," René said, "and since you can't, or won't, do anything, I'll do what has to be done myself."

"Roissy—she would never agree," O said.

"No? Well then," René said, "they'll end up taking her there by force."

That same evening, after it had grown dark, with Jacqueline in bed and O having drawn back the sheet to look at her by the light of the lamp, after having told her "René is in love with you"—for O did tell her that, and told it to her right away—O, who at the idea of seeing this body so fragile and slender belabored by the lash, this tight sex wrenched open, this pure mouth screaming, and the down on those cheeks streaked with tears, had, a month earlier, been horrified, repeated René's last remark to herself, and was happy.

148

With Jacqueline gone and probably not due back until the beginning of August, if the film she was working in was completed by then, nothing further was keeping O in Paris. July was around the corner, all the gardens were a riot of crimson geraniums, all the awnings were lowered against the noonday glare, René was complaining that he couldn't get out of having to make a trip to Scotland. For a moment O had hopes that he'd take her along. But apart from the fact that he never took her to see his family, she knew that he would surrender her to Sir Stephen if Sir Stephen asked for her.

Sir Stephen declared that he would come to get her the day René took the plane for London. She was on vacation.

"We're going to Anne-Marie's," he said. "She expects you. Don't bother about luggage, you won't need anything."

They went to see Anne-Marie—not to the Observatoire apartment where they'd first met but to a little cottage at the end of a big garden, situated on the edge of the Fontainbleau Forest. Since the first day it had been given to her, O had worn the whalebone corset that Anne-Marie had deemed so necessary: each day she laced it tighter, and by now one could almost circle O's waist with one's ten fingers: Anne-Marie would be pleased.

When they arrived it was two in the afternoon, the house seemed asleep, and in answer to the doorbell, the dog barked faintly: a big shaggy sheepdog who sniffed O's knees under her skirt. Anne-Marie was reclining on a chaise-lounge under a copper beech at the far end of the lawn which, in a corner of the garden, faced the windows of her bedroom. She didn't get up.

"Here's O," said Sir Stephen. "You know what's to be

149

done with her. When will she be ready?"

Anne-Marie gazed at O. "You mean you haven't told her? Well, I might as well start right now. You ought to allow ten days. I suppose you want to put the rings and the mark on yourself. Come back in two weeks. Then everything should be in order two weeks after that."

O wanted to say something, to ask a question. "One moment, O," said Anne-Marie, "go to your room—it's the one in front—and get undressed. Keep only your sandals on. Then come back here."

The room was empty, a big white room with heavy purple drapes. O put her bag, her gloves, her clothes on a little chair near the closet door. There was no mirror. She re-emerged slowly, dazzled by the sun before regaining the shade of the copper beech. Sir Stephen was still standing in front of Anne-Marie, who as before was lying down, the dog curled up at her feet. Anne-Marie's black and gray hair shone as if oiled, her blue eyes looked black. She was dressed in white, had a patent-leather belt around her waist, and was wearing patent-leather sandals; her toenails were painted the same bright red as her fingernails.

"O," she said, " kneel in front of Sir Stephen."

O knelt, her hands behind her back, her nipples trembling. The dog looked as though it was about to spring at her.

"Here, Turk," said Anne-Marie. "O, do you consent to wear the rings and the insignia Sir Stephen desires to have you wear, without knowing in advance how they will be placed on you?"

"Yes," said O.

"Then I shall see Sir Stephen to his car. Stay here."

Sir Stephen bent and took O's breasts in his hands while

Anne-Marie was getting up from her chaise-lounge. He kissed her on the mouth, murmured: "Are you mine, O, are you really mine?" and then he left her to follow Anne-Marie. The gate banged, Anne-Marie returned. O was sitting on her heels and had her hands on her knees, like an Egyptian statue.

Three other girls lived in the house, each of whom had a room on the second floor; the one O was given was on the ground floor, next to Anne-Marie's. Anne-Marie called up to the girls, telling them to come down to the garden. All three, like O, were naked. In this house of women, carefully hidden by the high walls of the park and, on the side facing a narrow dirt road, by shuttered windows, only Anne-Marie and her servants wore clothing: a cook and two housemaids, all of whom were older than Anne-Marie, severe in their black alpaca skirts and starched aprons.

"Her name is O," said Anne-Marie, who had sat down again. "Bring her over here, I want to have a closer look at her." Two of the girls—both brunettes, their hair as dark as the fleece on their sexes, their nipples long and almost violet—helped O to her feet. The other girl was small, chubby, had red hair, and below the somewhat chalky skin of her bosom a terrifying network of greenish veins. The two girls pushed O almost on top of Anne-Marie, who pointed a finger at the three dark zig-zagging stripes on the front of her thighs, welts which were duplicated on her buttocks. "Who whipped you?" she asked. "Sir Stephen?"

"Yes." said O.

"With what, and when?"

"Three days ago, with a riding crop."

"Starting tomorrow, you'll not be whipped for a month. But you will be today, to mark your arrival, as soon as I've finished examining you. Sir Stephen has never whipped the inside of your thighs, your legs spread wide? No? Men never know how to. Well, we'll attend to all that in due time. Now show me your waist. Ah, that's better, isn't it?"

Anne-Marie kneaded O's smooth waist, pressed with her thumbs, then sent the little red-head to fetch another corset, and had it put on O. It too was made of black nylon, but was so stoutly whaleboned and so narrow that one might have thought of it as a very wide leather belt. No garter straps were attached to it. One of the dark-haired girls laced it up, and Anne-Marie ordered her to draw it in as tight as possible.

"That hurts terribly," O said.

"That's the whole point," said Anne-Marie, "and that is why you are much more beautiful now. But you didn't tighten yours enough. From now on you'll wear this every day. Now tell me how Sir Stephen preferred to use you. I need to know."

She had seized with one hand O's womb, and O could not reply. Two of the girls were seated on the ground; the third girl, one of the dark-haired ones, was seated at the foot of Anne-Marie's chaise-lounge.

"Girls," she said, "turn her around, let me see her behind."

O was turned around, bent over, and the two girls pried her open.

"Of course," Anne-Marie said, "you've no need to reply. You'll have to be marked there, on the buttocks. Get up. We'll put on your bracelets, Colette will bring the box, we'll draw lots to see who will do the whipping; Colette, go get the box and bring the disks. Then we'll go into the music room."

Colette was the taller of the two brunettes, the other's

name was Claire, and the little redhead was Yvonne. O had not previously noticed that all three wore, as at Roissy, a leather collar and leather bracelets on their wrists. They were also wearing similar bracelets on the ankles.

When Yvonne had selected suitable bracelets for O and put them on, Anne-Marie handed O four numbered metal disks, and told her to give one to each of them without looking at the numbers. O handed out the disks. Each of the three girls looked at hers, no one spoke, waiting for Anne-Marie to speak.

"I have two," said Anne-Marie. "Who has one?"

Colette had one.

"Take O away, she's yours."

Colette seized O's arms, brought her hands around behind her back, fastened the two wrist bracelets together, and pushed her ahead of her. At the threshold of a French door, which opened into a little wing that formed an "L" with the main part of the building, Yvonne, who was preceding them, removed O's sandals. The window of the French door lightened a room which, at the back, was a raised rotunda; the ceiling, a shallow cupola, was supported, at the entrance to the circular niche, by two slender columns about two yards apart. Four steps led up to the rotunda, where a rounded floor projected into the room itself. Like the rest of the room, it was covered with a red felt carpet. The walls were white, the window curtains red, the curved divans and the couches, set in a semicircle facing the rotunda, were upholstered in the same red felt on the floor. In the rectangular part of the room there was a fireplace which was wider than it was deep, and opposite this a large combination radio and record player, on both sides of which, to the left and right, was a record library stacked on shelves. This

153

explained why the room was called the music room. A door near the fireplace communicated directly with Anne-Marie's bedroom. The identical door on the other side led into a closet. Except for the sofas and the radio-record player, the room was bare of furniture.

While Colette had O sit down on the edge of the platform—which, at the center, resembled a stage, the steps being to right and left of the columns—the two other girls closed the French doors after having closed the Venetian blinds slightly. Surprised, O at that point noticed that it was a double door, and Anne-Marie, who was laughing, said:

"That's so that the whole neighborhood can't hear your screams. The walls are also padded—nothing of what goes on here can be heard outside. Now, lie down."

She grasped her shoulders, thrust her down on the red felt, then pulled her slightly forward; O's hands clutched the edge of the stage—she felt she was about to fall—Yvonne fastened each of them to a ring, and her buttocks were thus suspended in mid-air. Anne-Marie made her pull her knees up against her chest, then O felt her legs put under a sudden tension and drawn in the same direction: straps had been slipped through the eyes in her ankle bracelets, and hooked to other eyes halfway up the columns, she was drawn somewhat into the air and exposed in such a manner that the only visible parts of her were the double openings of her belly and behind, drawn violently open. Anne-Marie caressed the inside of her thighs.

"This is the part of the body where the skin is most tender," she said. "Don't spoil it, Colette. Go easy."

Colette was standing over her, straddling her waist, and through the bridge formed by her dark legs O saw the cords of the whip she was holding in her hand. At the first strokes,

154

which burned her belly, O moaned. Colette, struck her first on the right, then on the left, stopped, and began again. O struggled with all her might, she believed that the straps were going to slice clear through her skin. She did not want to plead, she did not want to beg for mercy. But Anne-Marie intended to drive her to beg and plead.

"Faster," she told Colette, "and harder." O braced herself, but in vain. A minute later she gave way to tears and screams, while Anne-Marie caressed her face.

"Just a little more," she said, "and then it will be all over. Just five minutes more. You can scream for five minutes. It's twenty-five past, Colette. Stop at half-past, when I tell you."

But O screamed no, no, for God's sake no, she couldn't bear it any longer, no, she couldn't bear it one more second. Yet she did bear it until the end and, at half-past the hour, Anne-Marie smiling at her, Colette left the stage.

"Thank me," Anne-Marie said to O, and O thanked her.

She knew very well why Anne-Marie had judged it above all necessary to have her whipped. That a woman was as cruel as, and more implacable than, a man, O had never doubted. But O had thought that Anne-Marie was seeking less to demonstrate her power than to establish a complicity between O and herself. O had never really understood, but had finally come to accept as an undeniable and important truth, the contradictory but constant jumble of her feelings and attitudes: she liked the idea of torture, when she underwent it she would have betrayed the entire world to escape it, and when it was over she was happy to have undergone it, and happier still the more cruel and prolonged it had been. Anne-Marie had correctly calculated both O's acquiescence and her revolt, and knew very well that her pleas for mercy had been genuine. There was a third reason for what she had done, which she explained to O. She felt it important to make each girl who entered her house, and who thus entered an entirely feminine universe, sense that her condition as a woman should not minimize the fact that here her only contacts were with other women, but, on the contrary, should be increased, heightened, and intensified. That was why she required the girls to be naked at all times; the manner in which O had been flogged, as well as the position in which she had been bound, had no other purpose. Today it would be O who would remain for the rest of the afternoon—for three more hours—with her legs spread and raised, exposed on the dais facing the garden. She would have the overwhelming desire to close her legs. Tomorrow it would be Claire or Colette, or Yvonne, whom O would watch in turn. The process was far too gradual, far too meticulous (as, too, was this manner of applying the whip), to be used at Roissy. But O would see how effective it was. Apart from the rings and the insignia she would wear when she left, she would be restored to Sir Stephen much more openly and profoundly a slave than she could imagine.

The following morning, after breakfast, Anne-Marie told O and Yvonne to come with her into her room. From her secretary she took a green leather coffer which she set on the bed and opened. The two girls were seated at her feet.

"Yvonne hasn't told you anything about this?" Anne-Marie asked O.

O shook her head. What was there for Yvonne to tell her?

"And I'm sure Sir Stephen didn't either. Well, here are the rings he wants you to wear."

The rings were of unpolished stainless steel, like the iron in the iron-and-gold ring. The metal was round, about the thickness of a pencil, the shape of each ring oblong, similar to the links of a heavy chain. Anne-Marie showed O that each was composed of two U-shaped halves, one of which fitted into the other.

"This is simply the test model," she said. "It can be removed. If you look closely you'll see that here, in the permanent variety, there are spring catches inside the hollow prongs: you insert the other half and it locks. Once locked it can't be opened. You would have to file the ring in two."

Each ring was as long as two joints of the little finger, and wide enough for one's little finger to slide through. From each ring was suspended, like a second link, or like the loop which supports the pendant of an earring, a disk of the same metal and as large in diameter as the earring was long. On one side a triskelion of gold inlay; on the other, nothing.

"On the blank side," said Anne-Marie, "your name will be engraved, also your title, Sir Stephen's first and last names, and beneath that, a device: a crossed whip and riding crop. Yvonne is wearing a similar disk on her collar. But you'll wear yours on your belly."

"But—" O began.

"I know," Anne-Marie interrupted, "that's why I brought Yvonne along. Show yours, Yvonne."

The red-haired girl rose and lay back on the bed. Anne-Marie opened her thighs and showed O that one of her labia, midway down and close to its base, had been pierced: a clean hole, such as a ticket puncher makes. A clean hole: the iron ring would just fit into it.

"I'll make the hole for you in a moment or two, O," said Anne-Marie, "there's nothing to it. What takes time is putting the clamps in place in order to suture the outer and inner layers, and attach the epidermis and the membrane.

It's much less painful than the whip."

"But aren't you going to give me some anesthesia?" O cried, trembling.

"Certainly not," replied Anne-Marie, "you'll simply be tied somewhat more tightly than yesterday. That's quite sufficient. Now come along."

A week later, Anne-Marie removed the clamps and slipped on the test model. It was lighter than it looked, for it was hollow, but O could still feel its weight. The hard metal, which was visibly penetrating the flesh, resembled an instrument of torture. What would it be like when the second ring was added and it hung even more heavily? This barbaric apparatus would immediately be apparent to even the most casual glance.

"Of course," Anne-Marie admitted when O pointed this out to her, "but did you understand what Sir Stephen wants? Whoever, at Roissy or anywhere else, Sir Stephen or anyone else, you too looking in the mirror, whoever lifts up your skirt will immediately see the rings on your belly, and, if he turns you around, the insignia on your buttocks. It's possible that you may someday succeed in having the rings filed off, but you'll never get rid of the insignia."

"I used to think," said Colette, "that tattoos could be very easily removed." (It was she who, upon Yvonne's fair skin, just above the triangle of her belly, had tattooed the initials of Yvonne's master in ornate, blue script letters which resembled embroidery.)

"O won't be tattooed," Anne-Marie declared.

O stared at Anne-Marie. Dumbfounded, Colette and Yvonne fell silent. Anne-Marie hesitated a moment.

"Well?" said O. "Go ahead and say it."

"Ah, my dear," said Anne-Marie, "I hardly dare. You will

be branded. Sir Stephen sent me the branding iron two days ago."

"Branded?" cried Yvonne. "With red-hot branding irons?"

From the first day, O had shared the life of that house, a life of absolute and mandatory idleness relieved only by monotonous distractions. The girls were free to take walks in the garden, to read, to draw, to play cards, to play solitaire. They could sleep in their bedrooms or take sunbaths on the lawn. Sometimes they talked together, all of them, or talked in pairs, for hours on end; sometimes they remained sitting for hours, at Anne-Marie's feet, in silence. Mealtimes were fixed; dinner was by candlelight, tea was taken in the garden, and there was something absurd about the perfectly natural and matter-of-fact manner in which the two maids served these naked girls grouped around a festive table.

In the evening, Anne-Marie designated one of them as her bed companion for the night; sometimes the same girl slept with her several nights in a row. She caressed her and had herself caressed by her, usually toward dawn, would then go back to sleep again after having sent her chosen partner back to her room. The purple drapes, never more than partially drawn, would lend a mauve tint to dawning day, and Yvonne used to say that Anne-Marie was as beautiful and haughty in her pleasure as she was indefatigable in her demands. None of them had ever seen her naked. She opened slightly, or pulled up, her white nylon nightgown, but never took it off. Neither the pleasure she may have tasted the night before nor her previous evening's choice of companion ever has the least influence on the following afternoon's decision, which was invariably arrived at by drawing lots. At three o'clock, under the copper beech where the garden chairs were grouped around a circular white stone table, Anne-Marie would call for the box and the tokens. Each girl would take a token. Whoever drew the lowest number was then taken to the music room and arranged upon the stage in the way O had been that first day. Then—but not O, who was exempted until her departure—she had simply to guess in which hand, right or left, Anne-Marie was holding a black or white ball. Black meant a flogging, white meant no flogging. Anne-Marie played the game with unimpeachable honesty, and if luck would so have it that a given girl was to be spared, she would be spared; or if flogged several days in a row, flogged she was. The torture of little Yvonne, who sobbed and cried out for her lover, was thus repeated four days running. Her thighs, like her breast criss-crossed with its network of veins, revealed pink flesh pierced by the thick iron ring, finally set in place, and all the more striking in that Yvonne's pubic hair had been entirely shaved.

"But why?" O asked. "And why the ring since you already have a disk on your collar?"

"He says that I'm more naked when I'm shaved. I think the ring is to fasten me with."

Yvonne's green eyes, her little triangular face, made O think of Jacqueline every time she looked at her. What if Jacqueline would end up here, lying on this platform.

"I don't want to," said O, "I don't want to, I won't do anything to get her here. Jacqueline's not the kind to be flogged and marked. I've already told her too much as it is."

But how well blows and irons suited Yvonne, how sweet were her moans, the sweat running down her limbs, what a pleasure it was to wrest that from her. For Anne-Marie had twice (but, until now, only for Yvonne), handed O the whip and instructed her to strike. The first time, during the first

160

minute, she had wavered; at Yvonne's first scream she had recoiled, but when she'd begun again and Yvonne had screamed again, this time she had been overcome by a terrible pleasure, a pleasure so piercing that she felt herself laughing with joy despite herself and had to restrain powerful impulses in order to slow down the cadence of the blows and not strike as hard as she could. After it was over, she had remained at Yvonne's side the whole time Yvonne had been kept tied up, kissing her periodically. She probably resembled Yvonne in some manner. At least, Anne-Marie's similar feelings for them both suggested as much. Was it O's silence, her meekness, that appealed to the woman? No sooner had O's cuts healed and were scarring over: "Oh how I regret not being able to have you whipped," Anne-Marie said. "When you come back . . . . Anyway, I'm going to open you every day."

And every day when the girl in the music room was untied, O took her place until the bell rang for dinner. And Anne-Marie was right; it was true that during those two hours she could think of nothing except that she was open, and of the ring hanging so heavily from her belly (once the ring was placed there), that ring which weighed so much more heavily when the second link was added to it. Of nothing except her enslaved position, and of the tokens of her slavery.

One evening, coming in from the garden, Claire who was with Colette, had approached O and examined her rings. They were still lacking an inscription.

"When you went to Roissy?" asked Claire, "Was it Anne-Marie who sent you?"

"No," said O.

"Anne-Marie sent me, it was two years ago. I'm going

back the day after tomorrow."

"But don't you belong to someone?" asked O.

"Claire belongs to me," said Anne-Marie, who had suddenly appeared out of nowhere.

"Your master arrives tomorrow morning, O. You will sleep with me tonight."

The short summer night waned slowly, until, toward four in the morning, daylight drowned out the last stars. O, sleeping with her knees pressed together, was wakened by Anne-Marie's hand probing between her thighs. But Anne-Marie wanted only to wake her, only to have O caress her. Her eyes glistened in the early dawn light, and her gray hair, shot through with threads of black, cut short and pushed up by the pillow, more straight than curly, gave her the look of some mighty nobleman in exile, some dauntless libertine. With her lips, O brushed the hard tips of her breasts, with her hand fondled the valley of her belly. Anne-Marie was prompt to surrender—but it wasn't to O. The pleasure on which she opened her eyes wide in the glare of daylight was an anonymous pleasure, an impersonal one of which O was merely the instrument. It mattered not at all to her whether O admired her smoothed and glowing face, her lovely, panting mouth, nor did she care whether O heard her moan when her lips and teeth shut on the crest of flesh hidden in the furrow of her belly. She simply seized O by the hair and pressed her face harder against her loins, and only loosened her grip in order to tell her: "Again. Do it again."

O had loved Jacqueline in a like manner, had held her abandoned in her arms. She had possessed Jacqueline, at least so she'd thought. But the similarity of gestures meant nothing. O did not possess Anne-Marie. No one possessed Anne-Marie. Anne-Marie demanded caresses without concerning herself about what those who caressed her felt, and surrendered herself with an insolent liberty. Still, she was tender and gentle with O, kissed her on the mouth, kissed the tips of her breasts, and held her close for an hour before sending her away. She had removed O's irons.

"These," she said, "are the last hours you'll sleep without wearing irons. Those that will be put on you very shortly won't ever come off." She had run her hand slowly and tenderly over O's buttocks, then had led her into her dressing-room, the only one in the house equipped with a three-sided mirror, which was always kept closed. But now she had opened it so that O could see herself.

"This is the last time you'll see yourself intact," she said. "Here, where you are so round and smooth, is where Sir Stephen's initials will be burned into you, on either side of the cleft dividing your buttocks."

"I'll bring you back again to look at yourself in the mirror. The day before you leave, you won't recognize yourself. But Sir Stephen was right. Go and get some sleep, O."

But her anguish kept O awake, and when Monique came for her at ten o'clock the next morning, she had to help O bathe, do her hair, and paint her lips. O was trembling; she heard the garden gate open; Sir Stephen was there.

"Come along, O," said Yvonne, "he's waiting for you."

The sun was already high in the heavens, not a breath of air stirred in the leaves of the beech tree, which seemed to have turned into pure copper. Overwhelmed by the heat, the collie lay at the foot of the tree, and as the sun had not yet disappeared behind the mass of the tree's foliage, rays shot through the outer edges of the one branch which at the hour cast a shadow on the table, whose marble top was gleaming with bright, warm light.

Sir Stephen was standing motionless besides the table; Anne Marie was sitting beside him.

"Here we are," said Anne-Marie when Yvonne had led O before her, "the rings can be put on whenever you like. She has been pierced."

Without replying, Sir Stephen drew O into his arms, kissed her on the mouth and, lifting her completely off the ground, lay her down on the table and bent over her. Then he kissed her again, caressed her eyebrows and her hair and, straightening up, said to Anne-Marie:

"Right now, if you don't mind."

Anne-Marie took the leather coffer she had brought with her from the house, set it on a chair, and handed Sir Stephen the separated rings, on which were inscribed O's name and his.

"Go ahead," said Sir Stephen.

Yvonne lifted O's knees and O felt the cold metal as Anne-Marie was slipping it through her perforated flesh. Just before snapping the second part of the link into the first, Anne-Marie carefully checked to make sure that the inlaid side was against the thigh and the side carrying the inscription facing inward. But the spring was so stiff that the two prongs would not go in all the way. Yvonne had to be sent to get a hammer. O was made to sit up and, spreading her legs, they perched her on the edge of the marble slab, using it as an anvil, first for one and then for the other of the female halves of the links, driving home the first and then the second for the male halves. Sir Stephen looked on in silence. When it was done, he thanked Anne-Marie and helped O down off the table and onto her feet. She immediately realized that these new irons were much heavier than the ones she had been wearing temporarily for the past few days. But these were permanent.

"And now your monogram—correct?" Anne-Marie asked Sir Stephen. Sir Stephen nodded in agreement and held O by the waist, for she was stumbling and looked as if she might fall. She did not have her black corset on, but Sir Stephen's grip was so firm, and her waist so slim, that she seemed ready to break in two. As a result, her haunches seemed rounder, her breasts looked fuller.

In the music room, into which Sir Stephen more carried than guided O, Colette and Claire were sitting directly in front of the stage. They rose as the others entered. On the stage was a large, single-burner gas stove. Anne-Marie took straps from a cupboard and, passing them around O's waist and knees, bound her tightly to one of the columns. Her hands and feet were also bound. Consumed by fear and terror, O felt one of Anne-Marie's hands on her buttocks, indicating the exact place where the branding iron was to be placed. She heard the hiss of a flame, and in total silence heard a window being closed. She could have turned her head and watched, but she didn't have the strength to. One single, frightful stab of pain coursed through her, stiffened her, and sent her screaming against her bonds. She never knew who it was had driven those two red-hot irons simultaneously into the flesh of her buttocks, nor whose voice it had been that slowly counted up to five, nor whose hand had motioned for the irons to be withdrawn. When they untied her, she collapsed into Anne-Marie's arms and had just enough time, before darkness closed in on her and before all her senses deserted her, to detect, between two great billows of darkness, Sir Stephen's face, which was white as a ghost.

Sir Stephen drove O back to Paris ten days before the end of July. The irons threaded through the left lip of her sex and bearing the graven attestation that she was Sir Stephen's property, dangled a third of the way down her thigh and, with every step, swung back and forth between her legs like the clapper of a bell, the inscribed disk being heavier and longer than the ring to which it was attached. The marks made by the branding-iron, which were three inches high and a half that in width, were dug into her flesh as though by a gouge, and were about half an inch deep. The lightest touch of the finger to her buttocks revealed them. From these irons, these marks, O derived a feeling of great pride. Had Jacqueline been there, instead of trying to hide the fact that she bore them, as she had tried to conceal the traces left by Sir Stephen's riding crop just before her departure, she would have eagerly sought out Jacqueline in order to show them off. But Jacqueline wouldn't be back for another week. René wasn't there either. During that week, O, at Sir Stephen's request, had several summer dresses made and some very light evening gowns as well. He chose the patterns which she could vary but not essentially depart from: one opening all the way down the front by means of a zipper (O already had several similar dresses), the other a full skirt which could be easily raised, a corselet which came up to the breasts, and a bolero which fastened at the neck. When you removed the bolero, the shoulders and breasts were bare. There was of course no question of a bathing suit: the irons would have hung below it. Sir Stephen told her that this summer she would have to swim in the nude when she went swimming. No question of beach slacks either. However, Anne-Marie, who had picked these patterns, knowing the way in which Sir Stephen preferred to use O, had suggested a type of slacks fitted with two long zippers, one on either side, thus making possible to lower a rear flap without taking off the slacks. But Sir Stephen rejected the proposal. It was true that he invariably used O as if she were a boy, when he didn't resort to her mouth. But O had noticed that when she was near him, he always enjoyed, even when he did not desire her, and as it were mechanically, to take hold of her sex, seize and tug at her fleece with his hand, open her and probe inside her. O's own pleasure in grasping a similarly moist and burning Jacqueline in her locked fingers, was a constant reminder of the pleasure Sir Stephen took in doing the same thing to her. She understood why he did not want to have to cope with an unnecessary obstacle in order to obtain it.

Dressed in the twilled stripe or polka-dot, gray-and-white, navy blue-and-white, which O had selected for a pleated sun-skirt and a trim-fitting, closed little bolero, or in more severe black nylon dresses, wearing hardly any makeup, hatless, her hair free, she looked for all the world like a well-brought-up little girl. Everywhere Sir Stephen took her she was thought to be his daughter, or his niece, the more so because he now used the familiar *tu* form in addressing her and she went on saying *vous* to him. Alone together in Paris, walking along the streets, peering into shop windows, strolling along the river bank where the cobblestones were dusty during that dry summer, they calmly came and went while passersby smiled at them the way happy people are treated to smiles. Once in a while Sir Stephen would push her into an arched doorway, or into some impasse, into some dark place from which emerged gusts of cold cellar air, and he would kiss her and tell her he loved her. O would hook her heels on the high sills of those little doors that are usually cut in the great porte-cochere doors. At the end of a courtyard, one could see clothes drying in the windows. Her elbows leaning on the railing of a balcony, a blond girl would gaze fixedly at them; a cat would slip between their legs. Thus they went strolling to the Gobelins, down the rue Saint-Marcel, up the rue Mouffetard, to the Temple, to the Bastille.

Sir Stephen once steered O into a miserable, brothel-like hotel where the man in charge at first asked them to fill out the forms, but then said that he guessed it wasn't worth the trouble since they were only going to stay for an hour. In the room the wallpaper was blue with enormous golden peonies, the window looked out onto an air shaft from which there rose the smell of garbage. Weak as the one bulb over the bed was, one could see rice powder and hairpins scattered over the marble mantlepiece of the little fireplace. On the ceiling above the bed was a large mirror.

Once, and only once, Sir Stephen invited O to join him and two visiting countrymen for lunch. He came for her an hour before she was ready. Instead of having her come to his place, he came to pick her up at the quay de Bethune. O had bathed, but had still to do her hair, to put on her makeup, to dress. To her surprise, she saw that Sir Stephen was carrying a golf bag. But her surprise soon vanished: Sir Stephen told her to open the bag. It contained an assortment of riding crops, two of red leather and rather thick, two that were very slender and long, of black leather; a scourge with very long green leather lashes, each of which was looped in a bight at the end; then a dog whip made of a single thick leather thong, the handle of which was of braided leather; and, finally, some leather wristbands such as those worn at Roissy, and some rope. O arranged them neatly, side by side, on the unmade bed. No matter how accustomed she was to these things, whatever her resolve, she was trembling. Sir Stephen took her in his arms.

"Which do you prefer, O?" he said to her.

But she could hardly speak and already felt the sweat welling in her armpits.

"Which do you prefer?" he repeated. "All right," he went on in the face of her silence, "you can help me first." He asked her for some nails. Having arranged the whips and crops in a decorative manner, he showed O that a panel of wainscotting between her mirror and the fireplace opposite her bed would be the ideal place to hang them up. He hammered in the nails. Fitted into the ends of the handles of the whips and crops were rings by which they could be suspended from L-shaped nails, so that one could take each whip or crop down and put it back easily without disturbing the others; thus, with the wristbands and the ropes, O would have, facing her bed, the complete panoply of her instruments of torture. It was a pretty display, as harmonious as the wheel and the pincers in the pictures of Saint Catherine's martyrdom, as the hammer and the nails, the crown of thorns, and the lance and the escourges in the painting of the Crucifixion. When Jacqueline came back . . . but this was also, in fact, for her benefit. She had to answer Sir Stephen's question: O could not, and he made his own choice: the dog whip.

In a tiny private dining room on the third floor of the La Perouse restaurant where figures out of Watteau in light, faintly faded colors on the dark walls resembled actors in a puppet theater, O was installed on the sofa, one of Sir Stephen's friends to her left in a chair, another to her right in another chair, and Sir Stephen, also in a chair, across from

169

her. She had already seen one of these men at Roissy, but she did not remember ever having been taken by him. The other was a tall young man with red hair and gray eyes; he was certainly no more that twenty-five. In two words Sir Stephen explained to them why he had invited O and what she was. Listening to him, O was once again astonished at the coarseness of his language. But, then, how else could she expect to be described if not as a whore, a girl who said yes, consented, in the presence of three men, not to mention the restaurant waiters who were still coming in and out, the meal still being in progress, to open her jacket and show her breasts whose tips were conspicuously painted and which, as one could very plainly see by the two purple furrows running across the milk-white skin, had recently been beaten.

The meal went on and on, and the two Englishmen drank a great deal. At coffee, when liqueurs had been brought, Sir Stephen pushed the table toward the other wall, and after having raised her skirt to show his friends how O had been marked and ironed, left her to them.

The man she had met at Roissy wasted no time: without rising from his chair, without so much as touching her, he bade her kneel down in front of him, take his sex and caress it, then he discharged into her mouth; that accomplished, he ordered her to straighten out his clothing and left.

But the red-haired young man, overwhelmed by O's submissiveness, by the sight of her irons and the lacerations he had seen on her body, instead of throwing himself upon her, as O expected, took her by the hand and, completely ignoring the waiters' knowing smiles, went down the stairs and, after hailing a taxi, took her to his hotel room. He did not let her go till nightfall, after having frenziedly, unmercifully belabored her fore and aft, for he was thick and stiff and

170

completely crazed to find himself all of a sudden, for the first time, free to penetrate a woman wherever he chose and to have a woman embrace him as he had shortly before seen that it was possible to make a woman embrace one (and as, up till now, he had never dared ask any woman to do).

When O arrived at Sir Stephen's the next day toward two o'clock in answer to his summons, she found his face grave and careworn. He looked older.

"Eric has fallen madly in love with you, O," he said to her. "He came here this morning and begged me to grant you your freedom. He said he wants to marry you. He wants to save you. You know how I treat you, O, you know what I am going to keep on doing to you as long as you're mine, and if you're mine you have no right to refuse my commands. But you also know that you are always free to refuse to be mine. I told him that. He's coming back at three."

O began to laugh. "Don't you think it's a bit late in the day for that?" she said. "You're crazy, both of you. If Eric hadn't come to see you this morning, what would you have done with me this afternoon? We'd have gone for a walk and nothing else? Just for a walk? Then let's go for a walk. Or perhaps you didn't mean to summon me this afternoon? If so, I'll be going. . . ."

"No," said Sir Stephen, "I'd have called you, O, but not to take you out for a walk. I wanted—"

"Say it."

"Come, it will be simpler to show you."

He rose and opened a door in the wall across from the fireplace. It was a door similar to the one that led into his office downstairs, and O had always thought it was the door to what had once been a closet and was now sealed off. She saw a very small boudoir, freshly painted, hung

171

with dark red silk; half of the room was occupied by a curved stage flanked by two columns, identical to the platform in the music room at Samois.

"The walls and ceiling are sound-proofed, aren't they," said O, "and the door is padded, isn't it, and you've had a double window installed?"

Sir Stephen nodded.

"But since when?"

"Since your return."

"And why?"

"Why what?"

"Why have I waited until today? Because I have been waiting to put you into other men's hands. Now I am going to punish you for it. I have never punished you, O."

"But I am yours," said O, "punish me if you like. And when Eric comes . . . . "

And when, an hour later, he was brought into the presence of an O grotesquely spread-eagled and strapped to the two columns, the young man blanched, stammered a few words, and disappeared. O expected never to see him again. But she encountered him at Roissy toward the end of September, and he had her assigned to him for three days in a row, during which he mistreated her savagely.

4

The Owl

*I*f O hesitated to speak to Jacqueline about what René very justly termed her true condition, it was because she no longer understood it. Anne-Marie had indeed told her that, by the time she left Samois, she would be a changed person. She had never believed that the change would be so drastic. With Jacqueline home again, more radiant and fresh than ever, O now felt it quite natural not to hide herself any longer when she bathed or dressed than when she had been alone. Jacqueline, however, took so little interest in anything apart from herself that it was not until two days after her return that she happened to enter the bathroom at the very moment when O, stepping out of the tub, allowed the irons hanging from her belly to strike against the enamel: the strange sound attracted Jacqueline's attention. She turned her head and at the same time saw the zig-zagging welts streaking O's thighs and breasts and the disk suspended between her legs.

"What's that all about?" she said.

"Sir Stephen," O replied. And she added matter-of-factly: "René gave me to him. He's had me pierced with his rings. Look." And all the while drying herself with the bath towel,

175

she walked over to Jacqueline who, completely nonplussed, had sat down on the lacquered bathroom stool; O came close, close enough to enable Jacqueline to take the disk between her fingers and read what was written on it; then, lifting the towel away and turning around, she pointed to the S and the H branded on her buttocks, and said: "He also had me branded with his initials. The others are whip marks. He generally whips me himself, but he also has me whipped by his black servant, the woman he has for a housekeeper." Unable to utter a word, Jacqueline stared at O. O began to laugh, then tried to kiss Jacqueline; Jacqueline, horrified, pushed her away and fled into the bedroom. O quietly finished drying herself, put on her perfume, and brushed her hair. She donned her corset, put on her stockings, her slippers, and when she opened the bathroom door she met Jacqueline's glance in the mirror; Jacqueline was seated at the dressing table combing her hair without seeming to know what she was doing.

"Would you lace up my corset, please," O said. "How surprised you look. René's in love with you—has he told you so? No?"

"I don't understand," Jacqueline said. And, revealing immediately what amazed her most of all: "You look as if you were proud of it. I don't understand."

"You will, when René takes you to Roissy. Have you started to sleep with him yet?"

Blood rose in a rush to Jacqueline's face. She shook her head, but the denial was so transparently false that O burst out laughing again.

"Little liar. Come, Jacqueline, my love, don't be silly. There's no reason you shouldn't sleep with him. And that's no reason for turning up your nose at me. Come, let me

176

caress you, I want to tell you all about Roissy."

Had Jacqueline dreaded a violent display of jealousy on O's part, or was it from relief that she yielded, or simply because she loved the patience, the slowness, the passion with which O caressed her? Whatever the reason, she yielded.

"Tell me the story," she said afterward.

"I will," said O, "but first kiss the tips of my breasts. It's high time you got accustomed to that if you want to be in any way useful to René."

Jacqueline obeyed, so well in fact that she brought moans of pleasure from O.

"Tell me," she repeated.

Accurate and clear as it may have been, and despite the material proof she herself constituted of the truth of what she related, O's story struck Jacqueline as completely mad.

"You mean you're going back there in September?"

"After we return from the south of France," said O. "I'll take you there, or René will."

"For a look, all right, but only for a look," said Jacqueline.

"Of course. You can go for a look," said O, who was convinced, however, that if one went it would be for more than a look. Still, she kept telling herself, if only she could persuade Jacqueline to enter the gates of Roissy, Sir Stephen would be grateful to her—and that, once inside, there would be enough valets and chains and whips to teach Jacqueline obedience.

She already knew that in the villa Sir Stephen had rented near Cannes, where she was to spend the month of August with René, Jacqueline, and him (and Jacqueline's younger sister, whom Jacqueline had asked if she could bring along—not that she especially wanted to but because her mother had been hounding her night and day to obtain O's permis-

177

sion)—she knew that the room she was to occupy, and in which Jacqueline would hardly be able to refuse taking at least afternoon naps with her when René wasn't there, was separated from Sir Stephen's room by a partition which looked full but which, behind a *trompe l'oeil* latticework and trellis, was transparent: by raising a shade on his side, Sir Stephen would be able to see and overhear everything that went on in the room as if he were standing right next to the bed. Jacqueline, caressed and kissed by O, would be within full view of Sir Stephen, and when she found out it would be too late. O enjoyed thinking of how she was going to betray Jacqueline, for she had felt insulted by the scornful manner in which Jacqueline had eyed this condition of a branded and flogged slave, a condition of which O was proud.

O had never been to the south of France before. The clear blue sky, the mirrorlike sea, the motionless pines under the high sun; everything looked mineral and hostile to her. "No real trees," she thought with a sigh as she gazed at these fragrant thickets, beneath which stones, and even the lichens, were warm to the touch. "The sea doesn't smell like the sea," she said to herself. She blamed the sea for washing up nothing better than ugly little scraps of yellowish seaweed which resembled animal dung, blamed the sea for being too blue, for always lapping at the shore in the same place. But in the garden of the villa, which was an old renovated farmhouse, one was far away from the sea. To left and right, high walls protected one from the neighbors; the wing where the domestics were lodged faced the entrance courtyard, while on the other side of the house, overlooking the garden, was O's room, which opened directly onto a second-floor terrace which faced east. The tops of tall black cypress trees soared past the overlapping hollow tiles which served as a parapet to the terrace; a lattice of roses protected it from the midday sun. The red tile floor was the same as in her bedroom. Except for the partition separating O's room from Sir Stephen's—this was the wall of a large alcove bounded by an archway and separated from the rest of the room by a sort of barrier similar to a stairway railing, with bannisters of hand-carved wood—all the walls were whitewashed. The thick rugs on the tiles were in white cotton, the curtains in heavy white-and-yellow striped linen. There were two arm-chairs, each upholstered in the same material, and blue Cambodian floor cushions. The only other furniture was a fine Regency bureau in walnut, and a very long, narrow provincial table of pale-colored wood, polished like a mirror. O hung up her dresses in a wardrobe. She used the bureau as a dressing table. Jacqueline's little Nathalie had been installed in a room near O's, and in the morning, when she knew O was taking her sunbath on the terrace, she would come out and lie down beside her. She was a pale-skinned girl, not tall, chubby but nevertheless delicately featured, with eyes slanting toward her temples like those of her sister, but hers were dark and shining, which made her look oriental. Her black hair was cut short in thick bangs that came down to just above her eyebrows and, in back, fell straight to the nape of her neck. She had firm, tremulous little breasts, and a child's still undeveloped hips. She too had come upon O by surprise, one day when she had dashed out onto the terrace where she expected to find her sister and where, instead, she found O alone lying on her stomach on one of the floor cushions. But what had revolted Jacqueline had filled Nathalie with curiosity and desire. She

179

questioned her sister about it. Jacqueline told her just what she had learned from O herself, assuming that Nathalie would be horrified, as she had been. But far from it, it in no way altered Nathalie's feelings. If anything, it accomplished the contrary. She had fallen in love with O. She managed to keep it to herself for more than a week, then, one Sunday afternoon, she successfully arranged to be alone with O.

The weather had been less warm than usual. René, who had spent part of the morning swimming, was napping on the couch in a cool ground-floor room. Annoyed to see that he preferred to nap, Jacqueline had joined O in her alcove. The sea and sun had made her blonder than ever: her hair, her eyebrows, her lashes, the nests between her thighs and under her arms seemed powdered with silver, and since she was wearing no makeup, her mouth was the same pink as the pink flesh between her thighs. To make sure Sir Stephen—whose presence, O said to herself, she would surely have guessed, noticed, somehow sensed, if she had been in Jacqueline's place—could see every bit of her, O took care on several occasions to flex Jacqueline's knees and to keep her legs wide apart in the light of the lamp she had turned on at the bedside. The shutters were closed, the room almost dark, despite the slivers of light that spilled in between the cracks in the wood. For more than an hour Jacqueline moaned under O's caresses, and finally, her nipples erect, her arms flung back over her head, clutching the wooden bars of the headboard of O's Italian-style bed, she began to scream when O, dividing the lips fringed with pale hair, set quietly and slowly to bite the tiny inflamed crest of flesh protruding from the cowl formed by the juncture of those fine and delicate little lips. O felt it heat and rise under her tongue, and, nipping mercilessly, wrested cry after cry

180

from Jacqueline until she suddenly relaxed, the tightly-coiled springs broken, moist with pleasure. Then O sent her back to her room, where she fell asleep. She was awake again and ready when at five René came to take her and Nathalie down to the water for a sail; they used to go sailing in late afternoon, when a bit of breeze usually rose.

"Where's Nathalie?" René asked.

Nathalie wasn't in her bedroom, she wasn't anywhere in the house. They went to look for her in the garden, she wasn't there either. René looked as far as the little thicket of scrub oak at the end of the garden; no answer to his calls.

"She may have gone down to the inlet," he suggested. "Maybe she's already in the boat."

They set off without calling anymore for her.

It was then that O, lying on her cushion on the terrace, caught a glimpse through the tile balustrade of Nathalie running toward the house. She got up, slipped on her bathrobe—she was naked, it was still warm—and was tying the belt when Nathalie, arriving like a fury, hurled herself upon her.

"She's gone," she shouted, "she's finally gone. I heard her, O, I heard you both. I was listening behind the door. You kiss her, don't you O? You hug her, you caress her. Why don't you hug me too? Why don't you caress me too? Why? Because I have dark hair and because I'm not pretty? She doesn't love you, O, but I do!" And she burst into tears and began to sob.

"Nathalie," O said, "be still, Nathalie."

"What have we here?" O said to herself. She pushed the little girl into a deckchair, told her to stay there, took a big handkerchief from her bureau (it was one of Sir Stephen's handkerchiefs), and when Nathalie's sobbing had subsided a

181

bit, wiped her tears away. Nathalie asked to be forgiven, begged to be, kissed O's hands.

"Even if you don't want to hug me and kiss me, O, keep me here with you won't you? Keep me with you forever. If you had a dog, you'd take care of it, wouldn't you? If you don't want to kiss me but want to beat me instead, you can. But don't send me away."

"Hush, Nathalie, you don't have any idea what you're saying," said O in a whisper.

Also speaking in a whisper, and slipping down and hugging O's knees, the little one replied: "Oh yes I do."

"Do you?"

"I saw you on the terrace yesterday morning. I saw the initials on you, and I saw all those black and blue marks. And Jacqueline told me—"

"Told you what?"

"Where you were, O, and what they did to you."

"She talked to you about Roissy?"

"She also told me you've been—that you were—"

"That I was what?"

"That you wear iron rings."

"Yes," said O, "and what else?"

"And that Sir Stephen beats you every day."

"Yes," said O again, "and he's going to be here in a few moments. So run along, Nathalie."

Nathalie didn't move; she raised her head to O's eyes, and met her adoring gaze.

"Teach me, O, please, please teach me," she said. "I want to be like you. I'll do everything you tell me to. Promise to take me with you when you go back where Jacqueline said you were going."

"You're too young," said O.

"No, I'm not too young, O, I'm fifteen. Almost sixteen," she cried, furious. "I'm not too young, just ask Sir Stephen if I am, just ask Sir Stephen," she repeated—for Sir Stephen had just entered the room.

Nathalie was allowed to stay near O, and extracted the promise that she would be taken to Roissy. But Sir Stephen forbade O to teach her the least caress, to kiss her even upon the mouth, or to let Nathalie kiss her. He intended to have her arrive at Roissy without having been touched by any hands or lips. On the other hand, since she didn't want to be separated from O, he demanded that she be present to see O caressing not only Jacqueline but caressing and giving herself to him, and also witness O being whipped by him or by Norah. The kisses with which O covered her sister's mouth made Nathalie tremble with jealousy and hatred. Cowering on the rug in the alcove at the foot of O's bed, like little Dinarzade at the foot of Sheherazade's bed, she watched every time O was tied to the wooden bedstead, watched her writhe and squirm under the riding crop, watched the kneeling O humbly receive the massive, upright sex of Sir Stephen in her mouth, watched the prostrate O spread her buttocks with both her hands to open the passage into her behind—she watched all this with no other emotion except admiration, impatience, and envy.

O may perhaps have counted too heavily both on the indifference and the sensuality of Jacqueline; Jacqueline may have naively judged that by giving herself so freely to O she was endangering her relationship with René. Whatever it was, Jacqueline suddenly ceased coming to O. At about the same time it appeared that she was holding René (with whom she spent almost every night and every day) somewhat at arm's length. She had never behaved like someone in love with him. She considered him coldly and when she smiled at him, the smile never reached her eyes. Even supposing that she was as abandoned with him as with her, which struck her as likely, O could not help thinking that Jacqueline's surrender did not involve her emotions. Whereas one had the feeling that René was completely, blindly in love with Jacqueline, was as if paralyzed by a love he had never before experienced, an uneasy, troubled love, unsafe, unsure of being requited, a love that lived in constant fear of offending. René lived, he slept in the same house that sheltered Sir Stephen, under the same room as O, he lunched, he dined, went out with, took walks with Sir Stephen, with O, spoke to them both: but he didn't see them, he didn't hear what they said. He saw, he heard, he spoke through them, beyond them; and, in a silent, harassing effort, like the efforts one makes in dreams to jump onto a moving streetcar, to hang onto the railing of a collapsing bridge, sought to find the *raison d'être*, the truth about Jacqueline, which must exist somewhere deep within her golden hide, the way there is some little mechanism inside the porcelain that makes the doll cry.

"Ah," thought O, "here it is, at long last, the day I've always been so afraid would come: the day when I'd become a mere shadow of René's past. And I'm not even sad; I only feel sorry for him; and I can see him every day without feeling hurt that he no longer desires me, without bitterness, without regret. And to think that only a few weeks ago I ran halfway across Paris to beg him to tell me he still loved me. Was that my love for him? Was that all it meant? So light a thing, so easily consoled? Consolation? But it does not even require that. I am happy. Was that all it took—that he give me to Sir Stephen, was that enough to detach me from him? Has new love come so easily in another's arms?" But then, what was René compared to Sir Stephen? So many ropes of straw, anchors made of cork, so many paper chains: such were the veritable ties by which he had bound her to him, and which he had so quickly severed. But what reassurance, what delight, this iron ring which pierces the flesh and weighs eternally, this mark that will remain forever, the master's hand which lays you down ruthlessly on a bed of rock, the love of a master who is capable of taking unto himself that which he loves without pity. And, finally, O told herself that she had only loved René as a means for learning how to love, for finding out how to give herself better, as a slave, as an ecstatic slave, to Sir Stephen. But thus to see René, who had been so free with her—and she had loved him for this freedom—walking as though hobbled, as though his legs were caught in the waters and reeds of a pond whose surface looks still, but whose currents move swiftly deeper down, filled O with hatred for Jacqueline. Did René perceive that hatred, through imprudence did O allow him a glimpse of it? She committed an error.

She and Jacqueline had gone one afternoon to Cannes, together but alone, to a hairdresser, then they'd had some ice cream on the terrace of the Reserve. Superb in a pair of black slacks and a black sweater, Jacqueline eclipsed even the sparkling brilliance of children, so smooth was she, so golden, so sleek and tough and so brightly fair in the blazing sun, so insolent, so distant and inaccessible. She told O she had a rendezvous with the director she had worked with in Paris; she said it had to do with some exterior shots, probably they'd go up beyond Saint-Paul de Vence to take some mountain scenes. Then the young man—the director—sud-

185

denly appeared, forthright and determined. He said nothing; there wasn't any need to. One only had to see the way he looked at Jacqueline. He was in love with her, that was obvious. Anything strange about that? Nothing; but what was strange, however, was Jacqueline. Half-reclining in one of those large adjustable beach-chairs, Jacqueline listened to him as he talked about times and places, dates to set, arrangements to make, and the difficulty of getting one's hands on enough money to finish the partly-completed film. With Jacqueline he employed the familiar *tu*, she replied by merely nodding or shaking her head, her eyes half-closed. O was seated opposite Jacqueline, the young man between them. It was very easy to see that Jacqueline, from below her lowered eyelids, was on the lookout for signs of desire on the young man's face; it was the way she always watched, when she thought that no one was looking. But the strangest thing of all was to see the uneasiness in her while she watched, the expectancy, her hands quiet beside her, the worry in that solemn face, without the trace of a smile, the expression of anxious concern O had never seen her display in front of René. A fleeting smile lingered for a second on Jacqueline's lips when O bent forward to set her glass of cold water back on the table, and when their glances met O understood that Jacqueline realized her game had been detected. Which didn't fluster Jacqueline at all; it was O who blushed.

"Too warm in the sun?" Jacqueline asked. "We'll be off in a few minutes. But red is becoming to you, by the way."

Then she smiled again, but this time, raising her eyes toward her interlocutor, her smile so tender that one would have thought nothing could have stopped him from taking her in his arms and kissing her. But no. He was too young to

186

know that immodesty can lurk within stillness and silence. He let Jacqueline stand up, shook hands with her, said good-bye to the shadow O represented for him, and, standing on the sidewalk, watched their black Buick move off down the avenue, between the sun-drenched houses and the deep blue sea. The palm trees looked as if they'd been cut out of metal, the strollers like poorly cast wax statues animated by some extremely absurd mechanism.

"You like him as much as all that?" O asked Jacqueline when the car had left the town and had climbed onto the upper coast road.

"Is that any concern of yours?" Jacqueline replied.

"It concerns René," O returned.

"What also concerns René and Sir Stephen and, if I've understood it correctly, a lot of other people too," Jacqueline said, "is that you are badly seated. You're going to wrinkle your dress."

O didn't stir.

"And, I also thought," Jacqueline went on, "you weren't supposed to cross your legs either."

But O was no longer listening to her. What did Jacqueline's threats mean to her? If Jacqueline were threatening to betray O for that venial sin, did she think that was a way to prevent O from betraying her to René? It wasn't that O didn't have the desire to. But René would not be able to bear learning that Jacqueline had lied to him, nor that she was making plans on her own that did not include him. Could she make Jacqueline understand that, if she kept quiet, it was to avoid seeing René lose face, turn pale over someone other than herself, and perhaps be so weak as not to punish Jacqueline? That it was, even more, from O's fear of seeing René's rage turn against her, O, the bearer of evil

187

tidings, the betrayer. How was one to tell Jacqueline that she would say nothing, without at the same time having the look of making a deal with her, you play ball with me and I'll play ball with you? For Jacqueline was thinking that O was terrified, with a terror that made her freeze at the thought of what would happen to her if Jacqueline were to talk.

From that point on, until they got out of the car in the courtyard of the old villa, they did not say a word to each other. Without glancing at O, Jacqueline plucked a white geranium from among those growing along the side of the house. O was close enough behind her to smell the strong but delicate odor of the leaves Jacqueline was crumbling between her fingers. Did she think that in so doing she could mask the odor of her own sweat, which was gluing her sweater to her armpits, was staining it darker there? In the red-tiled, whitewashed living room, René was alone.

"You're late," he said when they came in. "Sir Stephen's waiting for you in the other room," he added, speaking to O. "He needs you. He isn't in a very good mood."

Jacqueline burst out laughing; O stared at her and turned red.

"You could have picked another time," said René, misinterpreting both Jacqueline's laugh and O's concern.

"Oh, that's not the reason," said Jacqueline, "but, René, you've no idea, your obedient servant beauty isn't always . . . so obedient when you're not around. Look at her dress. See how rumpled it is."

O was standing in the center of the room, facing René. He told her to turn around. She couldn't, she was rooted to the spot.

"She also has a way of crossing her legs," Jacqueline continued, "but, of course, that doesn't show. Nor does the way she accosts young men."

"That's not true!" O cried. "You're the one who picks up young men," and she rushed toward Jacqueline. René caught her hand just as it was about to strike Jacqueline, and she was struggling in its grip for the pleasure of feeling less strong than he, of being at his mercy, when, lifting her head, she caught sight of Sir Stephen in the doorway, staring at her. Jacqueline had thrown herself back onto the couch, her little face hardened from fear and anger, and O sensed that, busy as he was holding her, all René's attention was focused on Jacqueline. She ceased fighting, relaxed and, stricken at the thought of being in the wrong in the presence of Sir Stephen, repeated, this time in a low voice, "It's not true. I swear it isn't true."

Without a word, and without so much as a glance at Jacqueline, Sir Stephen gestured to René to release O, and to O to leave the room. He followed her; but, on the other side of the door, immediately wedged against the wall, her sex and breasts seized by Sir Stephen, her mouth forced open by his insistent tongue, O moaned with happiness and deliverance. The tips of her breasts stiffened beneath Sir Stephen's hand, and he probed his other hand so roughly into her belly that she thought she might faint. Would she ever dare tell him that no pleasure, no joy, nothing she even imagined ever approached the happiness she felt at the way he used her with such utter freedom, at the idea that he knew there were no precautions, no limits in the manner with which he sought his pleasure in her body. Her certainty that when he touched her, whether to caress or beat her, that when he ordered her to do something it was solely because he wanted her to do it for his pleasure and his pleasure alone, the

189

certainty that he made allowances for nothing, was concerned with nothing but his own desire, so overwhelmed O that, every time she had proof of it, and often even when she simply thought about it, a cape of fire, a burning breastplate extending from her shoulders to her knees seemed to descend upon her. As she was standing there pinned against the wall, eyes shut, murmuring "I love you," when there was breath in her to murmur, Sir Stephen's hands, cool as the waters of a bubbling spring in contact with the fire consuming her from head to toe, burned her still more. He quit her gently, smoothing the skirt down over her moist thighs, shutting the bolero over her quivering breasts.

"Come, O, I need you."

Then O, opening her eyes, suddenly saw that there was someone else there. This large, bare whitewashed room, in every respect similar to the living room, also opened onto the garden, and onto the terrace between the house and the garden. Seated in a wicker chair, a cigarette between his lips, a sort of giant, his head shaved and his enormous belly stretching his shirt open and also clearly stretching the top of his trousers, was staring at O. He rose and moved toward Sir Stephen, who was pushing O before him. O then saw, hanging from the end of a watch-chain, the Roissy emblem. However, Sir Stephen introduced him politely to O, presenting him as "the Commander" without giving his last name; and for the first time since she'd had any contact with a member of the Roissy brotherhood (with the exception of Sir Stephen), she found, to her surprise, her hand being kissed.

All three of them returned to the room, leaving the door open; Sir Stephen went to the fireplace in the corner and rang. On the Chinese table next to the sofa O saw a bottle of whisky, some soda water, and glasses. So he had not rung for drinks to be brought. She also noticed a large white cardboard carton sitting on the floor near the fireplace. The Roissy man had sat down in another wicker chair; Sir Stephen was half-seated on the edge of the round table, pensive, one leg swaying. O, who had been motioned toward the sofa, had, in sitting, obediently raised her skirt: under her thighs she felt the soft prickly cotton of the Provençal upholstery. It was Norah who entered. Sir Stephen ordered her to undress O and to take her clothing away. O let the woman remove her bolero, her dress, the whaleboned belt that constricted her waist, and her sandals. As soon as O was naked, Norah left; and O, once again under the sway of Roissy robotlike obedience to the rule, certain that Sir Stephen desired nothing from her but absolute docility, remained standing in the middle of the room, her eyes lowered, so that she sensed rather than actually saw Nathalie slip in through the open French door, like Jacqueline dressed in black, barefoot and silent. Sir Stephen had probably made some previous explanation about who Nathalie was and what she was doing here; at any rate, now he did no more than mention her name to his visitor, who posed no questions, and ask the girl to pour the drinks. As soon as they had been given their whisky, their soda water, and their ice (and in the silence, the clink of the ice cubes against the glasses made a tremendous racket), the Commander, glass in hand, got up from his wicker chair, where he had remained seated while Norah had undressed O, and approached her. O thought that he was going to take her belly or breast in his free hand. But he did not touch her; he simply came up and took a long close look at her, from her parted lips to her parted knees. He circled her, inspecting her breasts, her

191

thighs, her buttocks, and this silent inspection, this gigantic body so close to her, overwhelmed O to such a degree that she did not know whether she wanted to flee or, on the contrary, have the Commander crush her beneath his immense bulk. She was so upset that she forgot herself altogether and raised her eyes toward Sir Stephen for help. He understood, smiled, came up to her and, taking her two hands, pulled them behind her back and held them pinioned there in one of his. She slid back against him, her eyes shut, and it was in a dream—or at least, if not in dream, in the twilight of a half-sleep born of exhaustion, similar to that one when, as a child, only partially emerged from anaesthesia, but still thought to be unconscious by the nurses, she had heard them talking about her, about her hair, about her pallor, about her flat belly where the fleece had only begun to grow—that she now heard the stranger compliment Sir Stephen on her, stressing the pleasant contrast created by the ample bosom and the narrow waist, and by the more massive, longer, and more visible irons than was customary. She also learned at that point that Sir Stephen had apparently promised to lend her to the Commander the following week, since the Commander was thanking him for something. At which point, Sir Stephen, pressing her neck between thumb and forefinger, whispered to her to wake up, to go to her room and wait there for him with Nathalie.

Had she cause to be so upset, and to be annoyed by Nathalie who, as though drunk with delight at the thought of seeing O opened by someone other than Sir Stephen, was dancing a kind of wild Indian dance around her, exclaiming:

"Do you really think he'll go into your mouth too, O? You should have seen how he was looking at your mouth. Oh, how lucky you are that people like you! I'm sure he'll whip

192

you: he looked three times in a row at the marks where you can see you've been whipped. At least, you won't think about Jacqueline all the time."

"But I don't think about Jacqueline all the time," O replied. "You're a silly little fool."

"No, I'm not silly," said the little girl. "I know that you miss her."

It was true; but not completely. What O missed wasn't, strictly speaking, Jacqueline, but the use of a girl's body, a body with no strings attached. If Nathalie had not been declared off-limits to her she would have taken her, and the one reason she didn't was the knowledge that Nathalie would be given to her at Roissy, in a few weeks' time, and that it would be primarily before her and by her and thanks to her that Nathalie would be surrendered. The wall of air, of space, of—to use the proper term—void that separated her from Nathalie, she yearned to break down, and at the same time she enjoyed being forced to wait. She told Nathalie this. But Nathalie didn't believe it.

"If Jacqueline were here, you'd caress her just like that."

"Certainly," said O, laughing.

"So there, you see," said the child.

How was O to make her understand—and was there any point in trying?—that, no, O was not all that much in love with Jacqueline, nor for that matter with Nathalie, nor with any girl in particular, but simply with girls because they were girls, the way one can be in love with one's own image—always finding the others more arousing and lovelier than she found herself. The pleasure she derived from seeing a girl pant under her caresses, seeing her eyes close, from stiffening the tips of a girl's breasts with one's lips and teeth, burrowing into her by thrusting one's hand into her belly or

193

a finger into her behind—from feeling her squeeze one's finger, one's hand, hearing her sigh, moan, cry—ah that! that she adored: if that pleasure was intense, incisive, it was only because it made her think constantly of the pleasure she could also receive from the girl when, in turn, her own muscles contracted around the finger, around the hand holding her, when she herself would sigh, would moan; yes, that too she adored, except that she could not conceive of giving herself in this way to a girl, the way a girl gave herself to her, but only to a man. It also seemed to her that the girls she caressed belonged by right to the man to whom she belonged, and that she was there only by proxy. Had Sir Stephen entered her room at some time in the course of the past few days while she had been caressing Jacqueline during the siesta hour, when Jacqueline was in the habit of coming to her room, she would, without the faintest reluctance or remorse, have spread Jacqueline's legs with both her hands, spread them wide for Sir Stephen if he had wanted to possess her instead of simply peering through the latticework as he had done. She, O, was fit for the hunt, she was a naturally trained bird of prey that would rise and strike and bring home the quarry, every time. And . . . .

It was at this point, as with beating heart she thought again of Jacqueline's delicate and so very pink lips behind the blond fur of her sex, of the still more delicate pinker ring between her buttocks, which she had dared force only three times, it was at this point she heard Sir Stephen moving about in his room. She knew he could see her, even though she could not see him, and once again she felt that she was fortunate indeed to be constantly exposed, fortunate to be constantly imprisoned by his gaze. Little Nathalie had sat down on the white carpet in the middle of the room, like a fly in a bowl of milk, but O, standing in front of the massive bureau she used as a dressing table, and above which she saw herself from head to waist in the antique mirror, a little greenish, and quivering, like seeing your image in the waters of a pond . . . it made her think of those engravings dating from the late nineteenth century, engravings showing women wandering naked in the subdued light of their apartments in midsummer. When Sir Stephen pushed open the door, she spun around so swiftly that the irons between her thighs knocked against one of the brass doorknobs and jingled.

"Nathalie," said Sir Stephen, "go downstairs and get the white box in the room where we were just sitting."

Nathalie returned with the box, which she set on the bed. She opened it and, one by one, removed from their paper wrappings the objects it contained, and handed them to Sir Stephen. They were masks. They were a combination mask and headdress intended to cover the entire head, everything except the eyes—two slits for the eyes, the mouth, and the chin. All sorts of masks: sparrowhawk, falcon, owl, fox, lion, bull—only bird and animal masks, scaled to human proportions, fully detailed, made of real fur or feathers, the eye-socket surrounded by eyelashes if the creature in question (such as the lion) had eyelashes, and the pelt or plumage descending to the shoulders of whoever was wearing them. A strap inside, when tightened or loosened, adjusted the mask so that it fit exactly one's nostrils and upper lip and lay snug against one's cheeks. Made of molded, hardened cardboard situated between the exterior facing and the inner lining of skin, the frame kept the whole thing rigid. Before the full-length mirror, O tried on each of the masks. The most striking, and the one which simultaneously transformed her most and also seemed most natural on her, was one of the owl-masks (there were two): its plumage in beiges and brown blended beautifully with her tan; the hood of feathers almost entirely concealed her shoulders, descending to halfway down her back, and, in front, to where her breasts began. Sir Stephen had her remove the lipstick from her lips; then said to her when she had removed the mask, "You'll be an owl for the Commander. But O, I'm sorry to have to tell you that you'll be on a leash. Nathalie, in the upper drawer of my secretary you'll find a chain and a pair of pliers."

Nathalie returned with the chain and the pliers. Sir Stephen pried open the last link on the chain and, slipping it through the second link O wore at her belly, forced it shut again. The chain, similar to the kind used for dogs—that was in fact what it was—was a good four or five feet long, and ended in a leather loop. O donned her owl-mask again, and Sir Stephen told Nathalie to take the end of the leash and walk around the room. Three times Nathalie paraded around the room; and O, naked and masked, drawn along on a leash attached to her belly, walked after the child.

"Well, it looks as if the Commander was right after all," said Sir Stephen. "He thinks all hair ought to be removed. But that can wait till tomorrow. For the time being, keep the chain on."

That evening, for the first time in Jacqueline's and Nathalie's company, in René's and Sir Stephen's, O dined naked, her chain drawn back between her legs, up across her buttocks, and wrapped around her waist. Norah alone served the table, and O evaded her eyes. Two hours before, Sir Stephen had summoned her.

It was the fresh lacerations even more than the irons and the brand on her buttocks which staggered the young lady at the beauty parlor the next day when O went to have herself depilated. It was in vain O told her that depilation by the wax method—consisting of pouring molten wax over the skin and, when the wax has hardened, removing it and the hair with it—is no more painful than a good beating with a crop; in vain she repeated to her, and even tried to explain, if not exactly what her situation was, at least that she considered herself happy; there was no way of reassuring the young woman, who remained both scandalized and terrified. O sought to soothe her, with the one result that, instead of being looked on with pity, as she had been at first, she ended up being looked upon with horror. Gentle as was the manner in which she thanked the young woman when the job was done and she was about to leave the little alcove where she had been spread-eagled on a table as though for making love, no matter how generous the tip she left, rather than feeling that she was leaving the place, she had the feeling that she was being expelled from it. Well, what did she care? It was plain to her that there was indeed something shocking in the contrast between the fur on her belly and the feathers on her mask, plain too that this Egyptian status aspect the mask conferred upon her, and which her narrow waist and long legs emphasized, required that her flesh be perfectly smooth. Only the effigies of primitive goddesses displayed so proudly and so visibly the cleft of the sex between whose outer set of lips appeared the crest of the finer inner set. And had one ever seen statues or goddesses wearing rings at their bellies? O recalled the plump red-haired girl who had been at Anne-Marie's, who had told her that her master only used the ring at her belly to fasten her to the foot of his bed, and also that he liked her to be entirely shaven, since only in that way did she appear entirely naked. O was concerned about displeasing Sir Stephen, who

197

was so fond of drawing her to him by her fleece, but she was wrong: if anything, Sir Stephen found her more exciting, and when she had put her mask on again, having wiped away the lipstick from her mouth and the rouge from her nether lips, and when those lips were so pale he caressed her almost timidly, as one does an animal one wishes to tame. As to the place to which he wished to take her he had so far said nothing, nor anything about the time they would leave, nor who the Commander's guests would be. But he came to where she was and for the remainder of the afternoon slept beside her, and later had dinner brought up to them in her room.

They left an hour before midnight, in the Buick, O swathed in a great brown cape, and wearing mountaineer's wooden clogs on her feet; Nathalie was there too, wearing black slacks and a sweater, holding O's leash whose leather strap was fastened to the bracelet the child wore on her right wrist. Sir Stephen was driving.

The moon was almost full, casting great pools of snowy light on the road, the trees, the houses in the villages they passed through, leaving everything else as black as India ink. Here and there a few groups of people were standing in doorways, and when this large closed car passed (Sir Stephen had not lowered the convertible top), one could sense curiosity stirring in the shadows. Dogs barked. On the side of the road lit by the headlights, the olive trees resembled silvery clouds drifting above the earth, and the cypresses rose like black feathers. There was nothing real in this countryside which night made imaginary, nothing except the odor of sage and lavender. The road continued to climb, but the same warm wind lay heavy on the earth. O slipped her cape down off her shoulders. She could not be seen,

198

there was no one left.

Ten minutes later, after having driven past a forest of green oak on the crest of a hill, Sir Stephen slowed down the car, drove along a wall, and came to a stop at the gate, which opened as the car approached. As the gate was being closed behind them, Sir Stephen parked, got out, helped Nathalie out, having told O to leave her cape and clogs in the car.

He opened a little gate. They found themselves in a cloister with Renaissance arcades, of which only three sides remained standing. The fourth side of the flag-stoned courtyard extended into a terrace, also flag-stoned. A dozen couples were dancing on the terrace, and in the courtyard a few women in very low-cut gowns and some men in white dinner jackets were sitting around candlelit tables; the phonograph was in the gallery to the left, a buffet table was set in the gallery to the right. But the moon was shedding as much light as the candles, and when it fell full upon O, whom Nathalie, her little black shadow, was pulling along by the leash, those who caught sight of her stopped dancing and the men got up from their chairs. The boy in charge of the phonograph, sensing something in the air, turned around and, taken completely aback, turned off the music. O had come to a halt. Sir Stephen, also motionless, was waiting, two paces behind her.

The Commander shouldered his way past those who had clustered around O and who had already brought improvised torches and candlesticks, to see her more clearly.

"Who is she?" people were asking. "Who does she belong to?"

"To you, if you like," said the Commander, and he led O and Nathalie toward a corner of the terrace where a stone bench, covered with cushions, was set next to a low wall.

When O had sat down, her back against the wall, her hands resting on her knees, and Nathalie had sat down on the ground at her feet, still holding the chain in her hand, the Commander faced the company. O searched the crowd, looking for Sir Stephen. At first she did not see him. Then she sensed that he was there, over there, reclining in a lounge chair at the other corner of the terrace. He could see her; she was reassured. The music had started again, the dancers were dancing again. At first, one or two couples danced their way over toward her, as though accidentally, then moved on; then one of the couples headed deliberately over toward her, the woman guiding the man. O stared at them through her plumage, stared at them with wide-open eyes, eyes darkened with bister, open as wide as the night bird she represented, and so strong was the illusion that no one thought of questioning her, which would have been completely natural, as if she were a real owl, deaf to human speech and mute.

Between midnight and dawn, which was beginning to grow pale in the east, for it was approaching five, as the moon waned, people approached her several times, came close enough to touch her, they formed a circle around her, then formed another, several times opened her knees, lifted the chain, then brought one of those double candlesticks of Provençal earthenware—and she felt the candleflames warm the inner sides of her thighs—to see how the chain was attached. There was even a drunk American who, laughing loudly, put his hand to her belly but, realizing he had taken hold of a fistful of flesh and also of steel, he became suddenly sober and O saw the same horror and loathing appear on his face that she had earlier seen on the face of the young woman who had depilated her; he turned and fled. There was also a very young girl, bareshouldered, wearing a tiny pearl choker, dressed in the kind of white dress that had two tea roses at the waist and wearing gilded sandals; a boy made her sit down next to O. The boy took her hand and forced her to caress O's breasts; which quivered under the cool hand; then he made her touch O's sex, and the hole through which the ring passed; the girl silently obeyed, and when the boy said that he would do the same thing to her, she listened quietly and did not appear upset. But even though they used O thus, even taking her as an example, or a sample, or as the object of a demonstration, not once did anyone speak to her directly. Was she then of stone or wax, or a creature from some other world, and was it because they thought it pointless to speak to her? Or was it because they didn't dare?

It was not until daybreak, and after, when all the dancers had left, that Sir Stephen and the Commander, awakening Nathalie, who was asleep at O's feet, had O get up, led her to the center of the courtyard, unfastened her chain and took off her mask and, laying her down on a table, possessed her, one after the other.

THE END